THE PATRIOT'S CREED

ALSO BY KRIS PARONTO

The Ranger Way: Living the Code On and Off the Battlefield

THE PATRIOT'S CREED

INSPIRATION AND ADVICE
FOR LIVING A HEROIC LIFE

KRIS "TANTO" PARONTO

CENTER
STREET

New York   Nashville

Center Street
Hachette Book Group
1290 Avenue of the Americas, New York, NY 10104
centerstreet.com
twitter.com/centerstreet

First Edition: October 2019

Center Street is a division of Hachette Book Group, Inc. The Center Street name and logo are trademarks of Hachette Book Group, Inc.

The publisher is not responsible for websites (or their content) that are not owned by the publisher.

The Hachette Speakers Bureau provides a wide range of authors for speaking events. To find out more, go to www.HachetteSpeakersBureau.com or call (866) 376-6591.

Library of Congress Cataloging-in-Publication Data has been applied for.

ISBNs: 978-1-5460-7647-6 (hardcover), 978-1-5460-7646-9 (ebook)

Printed in the United States of America

LSC-C

10   9   8   7   6   5   4   3   2   1

For my wife, Tanya Paronto, who is stronger than I am For our children, KJP, ARP, and CBP, who inspire me to do my best, For my parents, Rita and Jim Paronto, who have been my example and my strength, For my brother Mike and my sister Jamie, who have never lost faith

CONTENTS

ARMY VALUES

LOYALTY

Bear true faith and allegiance to the US Constitution, the Army, your unit and other Soldiers. Bearing true faith and allegiance is a matter of believing in and devoting yourself to something or someone. A loyal Soldier is one who supports the leadership and stands up for fellow Soldiers. By wearing the uniform of the U.S. Army you are expressing your loyalty. And by doing your share, you show your loyalty to your unit.

DUTY

Fulfill your obligations. Doing your duty means more than carrying out your assigned tasks. Duty means being able to accomplish tasks as part of a team. The work of the U.S. Army is a complex combination of missions, tasks and responsibilities—all in constant motion. Our work entails building one assignment onto another. You fulfill your obligations as a part of your unit every time you resist the temptation to take "shortcuts" that might undermine the integrity of the final product.

RESPECT

Treat people as they should be treated. In the Soldier's Code, we pledge to "treat others with dignity and respect while expecting others to do the same." Respect is what allows us to appreciate the best in other people. Respect is trusting that all people have done their jobs and fulfilled their duty. And self-respect is a vital ingredient with the Army value of respect, which results from knowing you have put forth your best effort. The Army is one team and each of us has something to contribute.

SELFLESS SERVICE

Put the welfare of the nation, the Army and your subordinates before your own. Selfless service is larger than just one person. In serving your country, you are doing your duty loyally without thought of recognition or gain. The basic building block of selfless service is the commitment of each team member to go a little further, endure a little longer, and look a little closer to see how he or she can add to the effort.

HONOR

Live up to Army values. The nation's highest military award is The Medal of Honor. This award goes to Soldiers who make honor a matter of daily living—Soldiers who develop the habit of being honorable, and solidify that habit with every value choice they make. Honor is a matter of carrying out, acting, and living the values of respect, duty, loyalty, selfless service, integrity and personal courage in everything you do.

INTEGRITY

Do what's right, legally and morally. Integrity is a quality you develop by adhering to moral principles. It requires that you do and say nothing that deceives others. As your integrity grows, so does the trust others place in you. The more choices you make based on integrity, the more this highly prized value will affect your relationships with family and friends, and, finally, the fundamental acceptance of yourself.

PERSONAL COURAGE

Face fear, danger or adversity (physical or moral). Personal courage has long been associated with our Army. With physical courage, it is a matter of enduring physical duress and at times risking personal safety. Facing moral fear or adversity may be a long, slow process of continuing forward on the right path, especially if taking those actions is not popular with others. You can build your personal courage by daily standing up for and acting upon the things that you know are honorable.

"The Army Values," US Army, https://www.army.mil/values/.

CHAPTER ONE

PUT IT ON THE LINE

BATTLES EXPOSE HUMAN BEINGS at our best and our worst. It almost goes without saying that the human capacity for destruction, violence, evil, and greed is on full display on any battlefield during war. But those of us who have actually been on the front lines are often blessed to have witnessed acts of profound sacrifice, heroism, and bravery. That is one of the reasons that I believe I have had the best job in the world. I am proud to have served as an Army Ranger and grateful to have spent a good part of my professional life protecting and defending America. It has been an honor to fight in battle for my country, and it is a privilege to bear witness to the sacrifices of American warriors.

People sometimes ask why a person would volunteer to risk his or her own life, over and over again. For me, the answer involves patriotism, love of my country and my fellow man, and gratitude for the blessings of my citizenship. I grew up believing that the United States was the greatest, most powerful nation in the world. Like many Americans, I used to take many of the rights and freedoms established in the Constitution for granted. But once I began deploying, I came to appreciate the comforts of home and to see that the threats to our freedom are real. That is why I am still willing to lay down my life today. It seems to me that a lot of the people who are feeling so grim about the state of our nation today are still taking our rights for granted.

When I tune in to the news these days, it seems like the United States has never been more divided. The criticism changes depending on who is slinging it—liberals or conservatives, Republicans or Democrats. But the overall feeling is one of angry pessimism. Political campaigns are negative, Congress is polarized, everyone is watching their own biased news source, and it looks like some people—and maybe whole nations—are trying to exploit our honest differences and foment dissatisfaction with democracy altogether.

But we aren't as divided as the media would have us believe. I have been traveling across the United States for a good part of the past few years, and I've connected with a lot of people who care about this magnificent country and our future. We have a lot in common. When we unplug from the news, most of us get along just fine, despite our differences. Of course we have problems. Of course the United States has problems. But Americans also have a lot of shared values, and I believe that many of our problems would seem less intractable if more of us would recommit to truly living by a few key, common values.

Army Values

When soldiers enter the Army now, they are taught that there are seven core Army Values: loyalty, duty, respect, selfless service, honor, integrity, and personal courage. Everyone in the Army is supposed to commit the values, and the principles behind them, to memory. To help us do that, the Army even created a mnemonic: LDRSHIP. These principles are the standards that all soldiers are supposed to live by, both on and off duty.

The Army Values are basic principles that, if followed, can help recruits become good soldiers with honorable careers. I'd argue that those values also characterize a good human being. The Army Values should be familiar to all of us. The Army didn't make up concepts like loyalty, integrity, and respect. But how often do we truly think about what they mean? How often do we live by them? How many of us truly prioritize the principles expressed in the Army Values in our own lives and consciously make them part of our own decision-making? And how often do we really live those values without expecting anything in return?

VALUES IN ACTION

My life was profoundly changed on September 11, 2012, when I spent more than thirteen hours on the ground as part of the CIA Annex security team, which responded to the terrorist attack on the US State Department Special Mission and the Annex, a nearby CIA station in Benghazi, Libya.

Our team of six former military special operators (Marines Dave "Boone" Benton, Mark "Oz" Geist, and John "Tig" Tiegen; Navy SEALs Jack Silva and Tyrone "Rone" Woods; and me, the Lone Ranger) had been hired to provide security for American diplomats and CIA agents working in Benghazi. Each man on our team had been deploying as either a serviceman or contractor for at least ten years, and we had each logged significant time in the Middle East. Our team kept in regular contact with the Special Mission, which we called the consulate, and we shared radios with them, but we did not have a directive to protect their staff.

When terrorists attacked the Special Mission compound, our team was initially told to stand down and to wait for local forces to arrive to handle the situation. But American lives were at risk, so our team acted against orders and fought all night, against tremendous odds, retaking the compound and defending attacks on the Annex.

By the time we returned to the United States about two weeks later, that day's events had already become politicized. As we saw the events we participated in mischaracterized by others for political purposes, I and the four other surviving members of our team became frustrated and angry.

Four Americans died during the attack: Ambassador Chris Stevens, Sean Smith, Tyrone Woods, and Glen Doherty. Tyrone and Glen, in particular, were our brothers. My teammates and I called them Rone and Bub. We felt that their sacrifice required us to bear witness to the circumstances that led to their deaths. With the help of journalist Mitchell Zuckoff, we set the record straight by telling our story, as witnesses, in the book *13 Hours: The Inside Account of What Really Happened in Benghazi* (Hachette Book Group, 2014).

Filmmaker Michael Bay made our book into a movie of the same name. You can read our book, or watch the movie, to understand the story of September 11, 2012; I'm not going to rehash it here. But the process of telling this particular story set me on a new path, and I wasn't sure that I wanted to be on it.

I was trained in the military to be part of a giant machine.

On a mission, I am just one small part of the highly coordinated and choreographed efforts of what might literally be thousands of people, most of whom I do not know and who don't know me. But we are counting on each other, and we know we can depend on each person to do his or her job.

Promoting *13 Hours* seemed, in certain ways, to be antithetical to the way I had been trained. Sometimes it was painful and exhausting to tell the story of that night, and a part of me felt like I was drawing attention to myself, saying, "Look at me, look at us, look at what we did." That felt uncomfortable. It still feels uncomfortable, but this new path requires that people hear and see me, and that is something I have to accept. My mission is always to accept and excel, to the best of my abilities.

I had good reasons for wanting people to know about the events depicted in *13 Hours*. Our team wanted to correct the historical record and to draw attention to the heroic sacrifices of Tyrone Woods and Glen Doherty, who laid down their lives for their country.

One thing I have come to realize is that being challenged is usually uncomfortable. I believe that God gave me a new challenge and set me on a path to fight a different battle after Benghazi. I am a man of faith. I accept that wherever I find myself in life is where God wants me to be. I do not have to like where I am, but I trust that God has me there for a purpose. I believe that it is up to me to figure out God's purpose in any particular situation, whether it is to learn a lesson or to be of service.

For the last few years, I have been doing more than telling my story: I've been listening to other people's stories. And I've come to understand that we are all fighting battles and that we can all learn from each other and lean on each other to survive them.

I am grateful for having been able to share my story, and the true story of my teammates in Benghazi on September 11, 2012, but the same social media tools that have helped me do that have also frustrated me. I'm not just talking about being attacked by members of the media or politicians who are serving their own agenda or passionate folks with alternate views. That comes with the territory when you threaten someone else's world view. I accept opposition. But I feel disappointed by a lot of social media. Sometimes, as I scroll along online, I imagine everyone hollering, "Look at me! Look at what I did today!" That's not why I want to be on social media. That's not what I want to read on social media.

I wish that more of us could connect through stories that inspire us, and just work at making ourselves better every day and not worry about who sees us, who likes our pictures, or how many people send us direct messages.

There are plenty of people out in the real world overcoming incredible obstacles. It's no surprise that a lot of them are veterans and patriots, men and women who have been willing to put their lives on the line for our country. If anyone is paying any attention to me, I'd like to steer them to some new stories. There are people out there who have done more than I and who have endured more than I, and they have wisdom to share. You are going to read about some of them in these pages. Maybe one particular story will resonate with you.

We can also learn something by seeing what heroic people have in common: the ability to move forward against any obstacles. They never quit.

I want to commemorate my lost brothers and to keep history honest, but I never want to be the guy who just sits around and tells war stories. That might sound funny, because telling my war stories has kept me busy for the last few years now. I'm humbled by the people who want to hear what I have to say, and I'm inspired by many of the experiences other people have shared with me in return. I'm grateful for the work I'm doing, but it's not the work I set out to do. I was trained to fight, defend, and protect people. If I could enter a time machine and return to the front lines, I would go back in a heartbeat. Many civilians do a double take when I tell them that I wish I could deploy again. Most veterans understand.

SAFETY AND LUCK

The United States is still a safe country. Walk around. Even our toughest neighborhoods are safer, cleaner, and more secure than most of the places where I have deployed (you'll read about some of them shortly). It is relatively safe to send our kids to school. It is front page news when there is violence in our stores or offices. We can drive to work and to the store in the first place because most of us have the opportunity to make money and to live well.

Our water and our air are relatively clean, and when there is a problem with those resources, we can raise holy hell about it and expect our governments and utilities to respond. Most people do not think of these aspects of our lives as luxuries. And maybe no one should have to consider them luxuries. But we shouldn't take them for granted, either.

A CLOSE CALL NEAR LITTLE ASSASSIN'S GATE

The guys who were contracting and doing logistical work in Iraq in 2003, at the beginning of Operation Iraqi Freedom, started out wearing gear made by 5.11 Tactical, a company that specializes in field equipment for law enforcement and public safety officials.

They drove around in light armored trucks, looking like the Americans they were. Many of them got hammered. A local guy might have been walking down the street with an AK-47, have seen a contractor's vehicle approaching, and just like that, our guys would become a target of opportunity.

By the time I got there, in the summer of 2004, we had figured out that if you were not clandestine, you needed to be seriously kitted up in order to walk around Baghdad with any degree of safety.

It is challenging to think of other people when you are uncomfortable, trying to maintain situational awareness, and trying to protect yourself. For example, in the summer of 2005, I was working at a checkpoint at one of the bridges on Haifa Street, a two-mile stretch of road in downtown Baghdad that divides largely Sunni neighborhoods from largely Shia neighborhoods. It was hotter than I imagine hell to be. Our checkpoint was near what we called Little Assassin's Gate, just outside the Green Zone. We were protecting the acting ambassador to Iraq, Deputy Chief of Mission James Jeffries, who was a high-value target to any terrorist operating in the area. We were trying to protect and get him into the safe zone, which required locking down specific areas and blocking intersections so that our guys could roll through. My team was charged with locking down this intersection. The intersection was dangerous under normal circumstances, but on that day there were reports of sniper fire targeting our area from across the bridge, where a huge building was under construction.

I was trying to control this area, but the motorcade we were waiting for was running behind. As we waited, I acted as a traffic cop amid the controlled chaos: the traffic was backing up, the drivers were getting pissed, and there was sniper fire I had to be aware of across the Tigris River near a bridge we called Bridge Number Two.

I was letting cars go through whenever I was sure they were not carrying vehicle-borne improvised explosive devices (VBIEDs). You can usually spot those cars because their suspension systems don't hold bombs well and they are weighed down real low, similar to low riders you might see in parts of East Los Angeles. In addition, they rarely carry passengers, just a driver.

I was paying attention to these kinds of details and trying to get Iraqis through who didn't appear to be a threat. I also had to be conscious of the other contractors who rolled up. Terrorists tended to target US, British, and Australian contractors, who were especially vulnerable if they were being held at a checkpoint, so I had to worry about moving them through as quickly as possible.

All of a sudden, I looked up and saw a guy standing in that building under construction, which was approximately seventy-five meters away, pointing a PKM, a Russian-made, belt-fed machine gun, right at my head. Time seemed to stand still for a second, and I felt like he saw me, like he knew he had me. He smiled and he winked. He didn't shoot. To this day, I don't know if he was a good guy or a bad guy. He could have been someone working security for the construction site he was standing in. I thought, "Holy shit, I just died." I knew I got lucky right there.

PICK YOUR BATTLES

Bad, scary, unfair things happen every day, all over the world. They might even be happening to you. Everyone is fighting a battle, and each of us has a unique story. It doesn't matter whether your problems are your fault. You can't let them best you. Many of us have a tendency to overthink our problems. We worry about all kinds of things that are not under our control, while neglecting the many things that we can control.

It is a normal instinct to want to feel good or even just to avoid pain and stress. Unfortunately, many Americans choose to chase away tough feelings with unproductive behavior. Too many of us become angry, drink or do drugs, spend money we don't have, eat too much, cheat on our partners, or do other risky things as a way of distracting ourselves from the stress of life.

Those so-called coping mechanisms distort your values and hold you back. I don't care if you want to call those behaviors demons or bad impulses, and it is your personal business if you want to try to understand why you are drawn to one vice instead of another. Too many Americans choose to live in a state of fear or regret instead of striving to be the best version of themselves. The truth is that whatever time you spend blaming yourself or feeling sorry for yourself is going to be time wasted. I'm sympathetic, because I've lost sight of my values and my best self more than once.

Everyone gets stuck. Everyone gets scared. The worst thing that you can do is let that fear paralyze you. Your worst actions and mistakes do not need to define you and they do not need to trap you. You are just a person who has lost touch with core values. You can choose to turn things around by making different choices, choices that are guided by values that make sense. It might be challenging. Change is hard. If it were easy, more people would do it, right?

It helps if you know who you are and what you want. Knowing that you need to change is important, but it's not usually enough. Making big, lasting changes requires patience, powerful motivation, effort, dedication, and guts. Having values to fall back on will help. If you are having a moment of doubt, it helps to have a set of fail-safe values that you can rely on, a kind of map to help you navigate the landscape of your own life. The specific circumstances you are facing might be out of your control, but the way you respond to those circumstances is 100 percent up to you. By the way, that includes what you decide to believe about and expect for yourself.

Life can be tough. The guys you are going to read about in this book are tougher. You can use their stories, and the Army Values they exemplify, to figure out how to hang tough when you are fighting your own battles. Soldiers need to be resilient; they need to be able to improvise and adapt in order to defeat an enemy. But this book is not just for soldiers.

All of us confront external enemies, but many times we also need to look at the enemy within. The Army Values document sets out principles that anyone can use to set the course for their own behavior. Sometimes it is painful to adhere to standards. But remember that pain is usually temporary and that you often have control over the way that you experience pain, which can make it easier to bear. If you can hold on, you will see that you can endure it and that you will be the better for it.

You get to choose. You can choose which values to prioritize. You get to choose whether to keep doing the same stuff you have been doing or to try something new. If the same old stuff hasn't been working, maybe you should do something different. But that is up to you. You can rescue yourself and be the hero of your own life. You can become the person you want to be. And even if you don't want to be in the Army, if you start to try to live your life according to Army Values, you're going to improve your life. You might even inspire other people to make positive changes in their lives.

You know when you are doing the right thing. If you make people upset while you're living the Army Values and doing the right thing, too bad. Hold your head high and stay the course. Loyalty, duty, respect, selfless service, honor, integrity, and personal courage: soldiers and first responders are willing to live and die by these values. You can too.

EMBRACING THE VALUES
START NOW

My Benghazi experience is a story about six guys fighting with some serious disadvantages and overcoming some long odds. The politics of the events of September 11, 2012, got a lot of headlines, but the story went far beyond politics.

I have come to realize that the idea of our overcoming is an important part of the story. My story has resonated with many people because we all struggle. Every day, each one of us has to get up and move forward. Some days are harder than others. The truth is that life will eventually improve, but you have to take steps to make that happen—even if you can only take baby steps.

As simple as that sounds, I know it isn't always easy. It is possible to take a step in the wrong direction, and it is possible to fall down. Moving forward requires that you get back up when you fall. In order to move forward, you need to stay focused on the present and on the future. Moving forward means not wasting your time getting mad about some perceived injustice that occurred in the past. Sometimes moving forward requires removing people from your life who are toxic or removing yourself from situations that bring you down. Moving forward means you will continually try to improve.

The guys you are going to read about in this book have faced some dramatic obstacles. Some of them are carrying scars on their bodies that let you know they have been challenged. It might be easier to understand a physical challenge than to appreciate one that is primarily mental or emotional. You can see someone who has lost his arm or watch a guy learn to walk again. You can't see depression or anxiety. But those are real struggles, too. My confidence has been badly shaken, I've been scared, I have felt weak and full of self-doubt. But I did not quit.

You need to have clarity about your values. Once you have identified the values that are important to you, you can set goals and align your choices and your actions with your goals and your values. It's that simple—and it's that hard. Because it can be day to day, even moment to moment, and you have to be honest with yourself about your strengths and weaknesses. Values are the unifying web beneath those choices, and values are what will give you the motivation to keep moving toward your goal.

"Never quit" is one of my mantras. But in order to use "never quit," you need to get started. Reflect on the Army Values, do an honest assessment of what you want and need to change, set goals that are meaningful to you, and go after it, piece by piece.

———————————————————————

CHAPTER TWO

WORDS IN ACTION

YOU WON'T FIND ME, OR MOST of the guys in this book, sitting around a circle in everyday life, sharing stories from the front lines. I might not like to talk about my battles, but I do like to read war stories, especially ones from before my time. *Charlie Rangers*, by Don Ericson and John L. Rotundo (Random House, 1989), has long been one of my favorite books. My dad gave it to me. It is the story of men who served in the Vietnam War in companies that were attached to regular units, like the 101st Airborne Division or the 82nd Airborne.

These guys were basically out there fighting the Vietcong on their own. These Rangers faced incredible disadvantages, but they used their wits, their skills, and a fighting spirit, and they relied on each other to win. *Charlie Rangers* does not shy away from the gory details of battle. I remember being intrigued by the mechanics of military fighting when I read it. At that time, I thought that a person would die if he got shot at close range. Maybe I got that idea from movies—I don't know. In *Charlie Rangers* there are several instances when Rangers continue to fight even after getting shot multiple times. That might have been the first time I got a hint of what the concept of "never quit" really means to a Ranger.

I grew up taking it for granted that you need to push through pain. My dad was a football coach at Adams State University, Brigham Young University, Oregon State University, and Colorado Mesa University. I grew up playing sports and attended Colorado Mesa University on a football scholarship. I thought that was pretty tough. I wouldn't understand true pain until I became a Ranger. But I started to get a glimpse of real toughness in *Charlie Rangers*. These guys were bleeding from bullets and still fighting. They willingly put their lives on the line, over and over again, to execute their mission. I really believe that I first began to think about the word *brotherhood* while reading that book. Rangers develop brotherhood by bleeding together.

Some people think that you can build brotherhood by going through a six-month course or academy, but there is a difference between the camaraderie such courses often create and brotherhood. You can build teamwork in a class, but teamwork is not the same as brotherhood. You might even suffer a bit together, as we did in Ranger School, during those times when we were not able to eat or sleep. But even though we were relying on each other under adverse conditions, we were not brothers in Ranger School—not yet. When I was a private in basic training, toward the end of the course we were allowed to go out to the PX for a couple of hours if we had earned the right to do so. A bunch of us might go out as a group and walk a mile to the PX together to get what we called licky-chewies—snacks. Maybe we were learning to know and trust each other in social situations, but what we were doing was essentially going out and having fun. Our true brotherhood developed only after we had put ourselves on the line and risked our lives to save others' lives, against tremendous odds.

Another Vietnam-era story that I admired was *We Were Soldiers Once...and Young* by Lieutenant General Harold G. "Hal" Moore, Retired, and journalist Joseph L. Galloway (Random House, 1992). That story, largely about the Battle of the la Drang Valley, and the role of the 1st and 2nd Battalions of the 7th Cavalry Regiment, is another detailed piece of military history right from the front lines.

Hal Moore seemed like a confident, likable guy who didn't take any shit. He was a lieutenant colonel and commander during the period he wrote about in this book, and when I thought about the decisions he made, I was deeply impressed by his leadership and his willingness to fight alongside his troops. He had to make some tough decisions on the fly, and he was skilled at adapting as his situation changed. It also seemed like he was willing to delegate and rely on others, but he didn't ask anyone to do anything he wasn't willing to do himself.

It's an interesting contrast to another book from the front lines that I also like a lot, *Black Hawk Down* (Grove, 2010), because that story takes place during 1993 in Somalia, and some of the people making critical calls were watching the action from a drone feed.

In *We Were Soldiers*, the leader was on the ground. It makes a difference, and I encourage everyone to read both of those excellent books for their authentic, thoughtful perspectives on selfless service and what it is like to be on the front lines.

Even though I loved *Charlie Rangers* from the start, I don't think I truly understood or appreciated its lessons until after I started deploying and began losing friends. When I think about how Rone and Bub died in Benghazi, I realize that *Charlie Rangers* verifies, across time and space, what I have learned about brotherhood. My buddies may be injured or dying all around me, but I have to continue to fight. Rangers never quit.

When I became a Ranger, I committed to putting myself at risk against any and all kinds of odds, even if they seemed insurmountable. The sixth stanza of the Ranger Creed says, "Readily will I display the intestinal fortitude required to fight on to the Ranger objective and complete the mission, though I be the lone survivor." That's not lip service. I took an oath to continue to fight even if I might be the last man standing. It doesn't matter if I might feel scared: I am going to do it anyway, because the people next to me will be counting on me, just as I'll be counting on them. It doesn't matter whether we like each other.

The person next to me might be someone I have never met before we marched together onto the field of battle. It doesn't matter, because if we are Rangers, we are going to be brave together. Rangers are willing to protect each other and to die for each other—that is brotherhood. *Charlie Rangers* helped me start to think about what Rangers actually did and what I might be signing up for.

I thought Rangers were the toughest thing out there, and I wanted to be one of them. Rangers had strength, endurance, and the ability to fight. I admired the scroll, the tab, and the black beret because I knew what they represented. (The Army has changed the berets for the 75th Ranger Regiment to tan today. I'm still trying to get used to it.) I couldn't wait to become proficient in weapons systems. I wanted to put on a ruck (in civilian terms, a backpack loaded with gear that might weigh between fifty and one hundred pounds) and march thirty miles. I knew I wasn't going to eat or sleep much for three months and figured Ranger School was going to be the hardest thing out there, but I was ready and willing.

It proved to be harder than I had thought it would be. One of the things I loved about it was that we did our own planning and did so much ourselves. We were learning every aspect of combat and small-unit tactics up to a battalion level. It was challenging, and even though it was tougher than I had expected, I was happy because I was pursuing a goal that had meaning to me. My suffering and my work had a purpose.

Rangers Are Not the Only Heroes

Being a Ranger is a hard-core choice, but it's not the only valid choice. There are so many worthy goals and different ways to be heroic. I don't have to look far to find examples from my own family. My grandfather, Joaquin Garcia, came to the United States from Mexico on a work visa before I was born. He became a citizen and a patriot. He came to this country for opportunity, and he worked hard to leverage what little he had.

By the time I was born in 1971, my grandparents had established their own farm. My brother and sister and I loved to stay with our grandparents on their farm. There, we learned how to hunt and we learned what it meant to work hard. We would wake up in the morning at eight o'clock and my grandfather would already have been out working in the cornfields for hours, planting, tilling, harvesting, and weeding. I could see him out on his tractor all day long. It was not easy work, and he did it seven days a week until he became paralyzed in a car accident in his midsixties. I never saw him take a day off before the accident. Our grandmother, Rose Garcia, was constantly in motion, weeding, cooking, cleaning, and working hard.

At that point, the farm was large enough that my grandparents employed farmhands and migrant workers, and my grandfather wanted to provide opportunities and assistance to other immigrants and their families. I grew up playing baseball in the fields of the farm with some of the children from those new immigrant families, and I witnessed how respectful my grandparents were to the people in their care. My grandparents had a mission: to make that farm work and to be successful, and they did not lose sight of it. They were grateful for the opportunities they found in the United States. I absorbed the example of their work ethic, their independence, their patriotism, and their sense of service and responsibility to others just by watching them. They set their examples through their actions.

I try hard to live up to the example set by my grandparents. For instance, I continue to work out very seriously because I know it is vital for the kind of work I do. When I am training or when I am out contracting, I want people to see that I maintain my body and my skills and I want them to trust that they can depend on me. I've been teaching over the last few years, and running a tactical training program when I'm home in Nebraska. I do miss the brotherhood and the work that I did when I deployed downrange (military-speak for working in a combat zone) in the Middle East, South America, and

Africa, so training seems like a way to keep using my skills, to keep contributing, and to connect with like-minded people. I'm very conscious of setting an example and instructing through my actions as well as through my words.

People sign up for these courses primarily to learn how to shoot or to improve their shooting. I shoot and train right alongside them. If it happens to be freezing in Omaha, Nebraska, or Tulsa, Oklahoma, or Sherman, Texas, or wherever I am teaching, you can bet I'm going to be sucking it up right alongside everyone else, with my gloves off and my fingers in pain. When other instructors are taking the lead, I am going to be doing physical training on the side, and I always let students know that they can work out with me in their downtime and that it will help with their training. If an instructor is sweating or freezing alongside me, I find it motivating.

No one is required to do physical training with me. Most people practice shooting in a static situation, where there is no stress or fatigue. In my experience, life does not usually require static shooting. If you are called to fire a weapon in a real-life situation, you will be lucky to be able to stand still and you will probably be under tremendous stress, with adrenaline coursing through your body. It is inherently dangerous to shoot a gun. If we can simulate a degree of healthy stress and fatigue through physical training and still teach someone how to get properly positioned on a firing line and shoot properly, I think that person will be better positioned for a real-life situation. So I think it is a productive challenge to help students experience duress, just enough to push them to overcome it, but not so much that it causes them to make mistakes that would put themselves or anyone else in danger. It's a fine line, because I don't want anyone to get hurt in training. But I don't want them to get hurt in real life, either. Being able to handle yourself during sensory overload is a great advantage if you have to fight. Training with the Ranger Battalion stressed me out to the point that—even today—my whole world slows down and opens up when I am in a high-stress environment. It is unlikely that anyone I am training will have to face the kinds of battlefields the Rangers train for, but they can be safely stressed to be tougher and better prepared if they are ever under intense duress or find themselves in an extremely stressful situation.

As an instructor, I am the example. I am a more effective instructor if I can do what I'm telling students to do, and if students see me working alongside them. I'm not showing off. I don't need to show off. I want them to know that anything is possible.

EMBRACING THE VALUES
FIND AND BE AN EXAMPLE

Sometimes it helps to clarify your goals by looking to the stories and examples of others.

Think about people you have admired. There may have been leaders, teachers, or mentors who have played a role in your own growth, or there may be real people whom you have observed from a distance, or there may be still others whose stories have been dramatic enough to be told in books or movies that moved you. It doesn't matter where you find them. Reflect on what you admire about these people and let that guide you in establishing your goals and clarifying your values.

It might be easier to keep working toward your goals and living up to your values if you are clear about where they are coming from. I feel blessed to have been raised in a family of hardworking men and women of action. My father has always been a man of his word, he has always had integrity, and he is the man I have always aspired to be. His example inspires me. My mother has never given up, even as she has experienced multiple health issues as she has gotten older, including a double mastectomy. She is still the head of the household and is one of the toughest people I know. My maternal grandfather's example helped set the values for my family and helped me understand what it means to be an American. He believed that Americans who work hard always have the opportunity to change and improve their lives.

I am trying hard to live up to the examples of my parents and my grandparents, and to be an example to others. I haven't always gotten it right, and I feel blessed to have had the freedom to learn from my mistakes. I have been lucky. Know that you are in good company: so many people are working quietly, fighting their own battles, trying to improve their own lives, and endeavoring to be of service to others. Their examples are instructive and inspirational.

CHAPTER THREE

LOYALTY

Bear true faith and allegiance to the U.S. Constitution, the Army, your unit and other Soldiers. Bearing true faith and allegiance is a matter of believing in and devoting yourself to something or someone. A loyal Soldier is one who supports the leadership and stands up for fellow Soldiers. By wearing the uniform of the U.S. Army you are expressing your loyalty. And by doing your share, you show your loyalty to your unit.

PEOPLE CONFUSE LOYALTY WITH AFFECTION. You do not have to like someone to be loyal to them. The members of our team in Benghazi did not always like each other while doing everyday work when we were deploying. Oz and I have very different personalities, and we often got on each other's nerves, but when we were under attack on September 11, 2012, we trusted each other and fought side by side. I respect him and would always want to have him on my team. There is no question about where his loyalty lies.

You do not even have to know someone to feel loyalty toward them. I feel loyal to the Ranger Battalion and to the special operations community, even though I don't know each member personally. I know that every man and woman in that community is willing to sacrifice themselves in the name of the United States and for the person fighting alongside them.

I was raised to be loyal to the United States of America. I wanted to protect and defend my country. In the big picture, loyalty might require that a person be able to put the sovereignty of this nation ahead of their own ambitions. But being loyal to the United States does not mean that you always need to agree with its leaders. When my brothers and I fought in Benghazi, our government left us to die. When some of us returned home, there were people in our government who tried to cover up the truth of the events of September 11, 2012.

And yet I am loyal to the country, to the flag, and to my brothers. I have redeployed as a contractor to protect American citizens and interests. My first redeployment as a contractor after Benghazi was to Yemen. I remember some people could not understand how I could return to the Middle East, or why I would want to continue to help, even peripherally, a government that had disappointed me in such a profound way. The answer is that I still feel loyal to this nation and I know that there are still great people here. I know that the United States is an imperfect country, but it is still the greatest country in the world, and I will continue to protect and defend it, as I was trained to do.

SCOTT GEAREN

Pararescue Jumper (PJ) Master Sergeant Joseph "Scott" Gearen has had one of those careers that is humbling, even if you don't know everything he had to battle just to do his job, which entailed putting his life on the line—numerous times—for the United States. Scott's loyalty to our country is inspirational and his fierce determination is instructive.

I have heard Scott describe himself as an ordinary guy with an extraordinary job. I would agree that he has had an extraordinary job, but I'm not sure how ordinary he is. Scott retired from the Air Force in 2002 as a master sergeant E-7, after serving twenty-two years as a pararescueman.

A lot of civilians know about special ops, and especially about Army Rangers and Navy SEALs. But fewer people know about pararescuemen, who are part of the Air Force and are generally attached to other special forces from all branches of the military.

Pararescuemen are the most elite rescue unit in the United States, and their motto is "That others may live." Called PJs—for Pararescue Jumpers—they are incredibly versatile medics who can SCUBA dive and parachute and are tasked with combat search and rescue and the medical treatment of soldiers. Pararescuemen are trained to rescue air crews who have gone down behind enemy lines, but their job doesn't stop there. Who else can be called if an airplane goes down in a desert, on top of a mountain, or in the middle of the ocean? PJs have helped to recover and treat civilians in humanitarian rescue efforts around the world and have offered support for NASA missions.

They don't get a lot of the glory, but PJs have been part of many of the military's most dramatic and famous recent missions, including parachuting into Panama with Army Rangers in 1989 during Operation Just Cause; the 1993 mission in Somalia recounted in *Black Hawk Down*; the rescue of Jessica Lynch, the soldier who had been taken captive during the US-led invasion of Iraq in 2003; and the recovery in 2005 of Marcus Luttrell, who alone survived an attack in Afghanistan in which three other Navy SEALs were killed (depicted in the movie *The Lone Survivor*). PJs have also been involved in many more missions that remain secret.

Scott was part of one of the most specialized units in the

military, working with a SEAL team from Dam Neck, Virginia, and an Army unit from Fort Bragg, North Carolina. Scott was assigned to both combat search and rescue units and was a team member in the establishment of the first Air Force special tactics team, which is known as the 24th Special Tactics Squadron.

He misses his work as a PJ. "I'd do it now if I could," he told me recently. "We wore civilian clothes and did real-world missions. I miss the camaraderie and the relationships you build, and I miss the things we did."

He laughed when he thought about his work: "Some stuff, like climbing mountains, trekking across glaciers, SCUBA diving, snow skiing down Mont Blanc, wilderness survival, and even jumping out of airplanes, are things people pay thousands of dollars to do. Of course, we were doing it in order to be ready to perform a rescue anywhere, anytime, day or night."

Becoming a PJ is no joke. To qualify as a pararescueman takes almost two years, among the longest special operations training courses in the service and one of the toughest. The vast majority of those who try for it drop out. Those who make it have to complete, among other things, the Air Force Combat Diver School, the Army Airborne School, and the Army Military Free Fall Parachutist School, and become paramedics certified by the National Registry of Emergency Medical Technicians. At the time of this writing, there are no women who have qualified as PJs, and there are many more men who have not qualified as PJs as well.

Scott is hard core, even among the elite group of accomplished PJs. But his path to becoming a member of that group was not a straight one.

Scott had graduated from high school in Tampa, Florida,

and was attending junior college while working as a butcher in a grocery store. The year was 1979, and Scott says he wasn't too inspired about getting up to go to work and school most mornings and was intrigued when one of his buddies suggested going to see a military recruiter.

"Those Guys Are Crazy"

Scott thought the military sounded exciting, and he was interested in seeing some of the world. The recruiter gave Scott some videos to help him learn about the possibilities for service. One of those videos showed a man who introduced himself as a pararescueman. Scott had never heard of a pararescueman. The guy on the screen put on SCUBA gear: the mask, fins, snorkel, air tanks on his back, the whole kit. Then this guy got into a big airplane. Scott didn't know it at the time, but that plane was a C-130. He watched other men in the video secure a parachute to the top of the tanks on this guy's back and hang some bundles on the front and back of him, and then the plane took off.

A few minutes later, the plane's doors opened, and this guy jumped out and parachuted into the ocean. Scott stopped the video right there, turned to the recruiter, and told him that he wanted to be a PJ.

"Those guys are crazy," the recruiter said to Scott. "Are you crazy?"

The recruiter explained that Scott would have to go into the Air Force with an open general status and that he would have to earn the right to try to become a PJ. It wasn't guaranteed. Scott didn't know what open general was, but he made the choice that day to join the Air Force and knew that he was going to volunteer to be a PJ.

Eighteen months later, Scott had completed the selection course, passed all of the physical challenges and psychological evaluations, and earned his maroon beret. The maroon beret that PJs and combat rescue officers wear symbolizes the blood sacrificed by fellow pararescuemen killed in the line of duty and their devotion to aiding those in distress.

Scott was assigned to the 67th Air Rescue and Recovery Squadron in England until 1983, when he got an assignment as an instructor in Albuquerque, New Mexico.

But he wanted to be more active in the field, so he applied when the Joint Special Operations Command (JSOC) requested pararescuemen from the Air Force. In December 1984, Scott was on his way to North Carolina to become part of the first PJ unit in JSOC. Scott's unit, which had a global mission that was shrouded in secrecy, was made up of combat controllers, pararescuemen, and intelligence specialists. Scott would soon find himself working with the most elite special operations units in the world.

He was right where he wanted to be.

"There is nothing like the feeling you have when you are just about to jump out of a perfectly good airplane, especially at night," he told me. "You feel the weight of all that SCUBA and combat and medical gear, and the engine of the plane sounds like a freight train while you're in the air somewhere over the ocean. You do get scared, but when the doors open and the cargo area fills with that rush of air, the fear just evaporates. You make a choice and you do your job."

On February 3, 1987, Scott was in Virginia, attached to a Navy SEAL team getting ready for a parachute jump training session the next day. It was an ordinary training day. In preparation for the jump, Scott reviewed a number of medical procedures with the guys on his team, including how to stop uncontrolled bleeding and how to make emergency airways.

Hitting the Ground at One Hundred Miles an Hour

The next morning was bright and clear, but cold. The ground was frozen and the temperature was in the low thirties when Scott and his buddies stopped at a convenience store to get snacks and coffee on their way to the drop zone where they would conduct their training exercise. Scott's next memory is of being on the field, rehearsing the drop as a dirt dive. It would be an ordinary jump, a beautiful one, into blue skies. This jump would be Scott's ninetieth. "I felt comfortable," he said. "The weather was great. This was going to be a typical jump, with all standard procedures."

Scott doesn't remember loading the airplane that morning, but he can imagine how it must have gone, because the process does not vary from jump to jump. When the airplane is loaded, a jump master communicates between the pilots and the jumpers in the back of the plane. When the plane gets to a safe altitude, the jumpers take off their seatbelts and the jump master begins using hand signals to communicate, telling the jumpers when to stand up and when to stand by. Six fingers from the jump master means six minutes; one finger means one minute. Everyone in the airplane understands what is going on. At 13,000 feet, the jump master yells, "Go!" and points at the open door. The jumpers exit in an orderly manner and do what they had planned during the practice dirt dive. Each jumper wears an altimeter on their wrist and falls to a predetermined altitude before opening their parachute.

During the free fall, the jumpers will "fly" themselves into a formation, sometimes a circle, and mentally note where everyone is. At a predetermined altitude, the jumpers break off, turning 180 degrees from the circle and flying away from the group for several seconds. The purpose of this maneuver is to get everyone far enough away from each other so they can open their parachutes without becoming entangled with one another.

"It's almost like driving a car," Scott said. "You learn how to fly your body, to direct yourself to turn away from the group and go into a delta, or tracking, position, with your hands back along the sides of your body. Your speed increases in that position and the air pushes you forward, which gets you away from everybody. When you are away from other jumpers, you return to your flat and stable position, facedown facing the ground, and you deploy your parachute by pulling the deployment handle."

Scott's jump went routinely—initially, Scott said. But then it didn't. "Another person, an Air Force team member, was still in free fall above me and determined that he didn't have enough time to avoid hitting me. He instinctively balled up in a cannonball position and crashed through my canopy. The impact destroyed my canopy, shattered my skull, and knocked me unconscious. I imagine that he crashed straight into my head and face, based on my injuries."

Scott does not remember hitting the ground at one hundred miles an hour. He didn't see the two SEALs in the air spiraling behind him, steering their canopies to get to him as fast as they could. "I don't remember anything after getting ready to jump," he says. "But I do remember doing that training the day prior with the guys on the team about first-aid skills and how to stop uncontrolled bleeding. I'm so glad they were paying attention."

Scott's skull was fractured on impact and he lay on the ground, blood filling his mouth and throat. Scott was convulsing and gasping for breath. The jumpers who had been behind him in the air rolled him over from his back onto his side. Men on the scene told Scott later that it seemed as though a gallon of blood gushed from his throat when they rolled him over from his back. Scott is still not sure exactly how many bones in his body were broken in the fall, but he had many fractures in his face and head and in his vertebrae, he was missing teeth, and his hard palate—which separates the oral cavity from the nasal cavity—was split all the way back to his throat. Blood poured out of the opening in his palate and filled his mouth, making it difficult for him to breathe.

Scott landed about a mile from the drop zone in a spot inaccessible to helicopters. So Scott's teammates used a poncho and tree branches to fashion an impromptu litter on which they carried him a quarter mile to the nearest opening in the trees. There, a helicopter landed, picked him up, and whisked him to Portsmouth Naval Medical Center. Scott got to the hospital about an hour after the accident, but the amount of blood he lost from the split palate was substantial: he needed a blood transfusion—he thinks it was eleven units—at the hospital.

"I'm Not Ready to Go Yet"

Scott had a powerful vision at some point in time between the initial fall and when his teammates first cleared his airway.

"I experienced the most peaceful, wonderful feeling. It's hard to explain it now, but I felt aware of my consciousness in a way I had not felt before. There was a softness surrounding me. I was surrounded in a soft white light, a field of energy or love. I'm not sure what to call it. I knew that I was leaving my body." Scott described this experience to me matter-of-factly. "There was a bright area in the right field of my vision, with three figures in silhouette. We were communicating telepathically as I moved toward them. I felt very welcome, and I was getting closer and closer. I heard a voice say, 'It's time to go now,' and I thought, 'But I'm not ready to go yet.' I turned my head away from the figures and they began to recede."

Scott is not sure if he had this experience during the fall, right after the impact, or sometime later. But he has no doubt that it happened. Scott was raised a Southern Baptist and grew up learning Bible stories and remembering to say his prayers, but he has had a different kind of faith since his accident. "God is real," he said, "and even though I don't want to die, I no longer fear death. It is not the end."

Scott's next memories are of drifting in and out of consciousness in a hospital. That must have lasted for two or three days, but he had no concept of time. "I knew something was wrong," he said. "I couldn't talk because of the tubes in my throat. In my mind, I thought I was trying to move my head. At one point, I thought I might be blind because I couldn't open my eyes, but then a doctor pushed my eyelids open. I remember realizing that I was alive but that something was wrong."

Scott was disoriented, and he didn't know the half of it. In addition to fracturing his skull, he had suffered a concussion in the fall, which knocked him unconscious. "I couldn't really see or move; I couldn't talk," he said. "At some point, someone put a pen in my hand and I wrote two questions: 'Will I see? Is my neck broken?'"

After hearing that his neck wasn't broken, Scott felt more hopeful. "Somehow, I knew it was going to be okay," Scott said. "I had a weird, calm feeling. I knew I was in the best hands possible."

Scott underwent a series of excruciating surgeries, including a procedure called a cricothyroidotomy, in which an emergency airway is opened, and an eleven-hour operation to reset his bones, affix internal plates and screws, and realign his face. His jaw was wired shut.

Because Scott could not be intubated during the reconstructive surgeries, his surgeons had no choice but to cut through the same spot in his throat during each surgery so that they could insert a breathing tube and thereby ensure he got the oxygen he needed.

Fighting for His Life, and Then for His Job

After a month, Scott was ready to try getting out of his hospital bed. He recalled, "I needed help to stand up, and it was kind of scary making that first step. I was still wired up and attached to IVs and very weak after lying down for a month. I walked maybe five or six feet that first day. It was [the] most I could do." Scott was a husband and a father at the time of the accident. His son was five years old, and he went to stay with his grandmother while Scott's wife moved into an apartment near the hospital.

Scott got out of bed every day after that and walked a little bit farther. After another month, Scott's doctors released him from the hospital on the condition that he would return every day for rehab. Three months later, the doctors took the wires out of his jaw.

As he fought—first for his life and then for his full physical recovery—Scott realized that he was also going to have to fight for his job. He didn't feel angry. "It wasn't personal," he said. "The military is a big system and sometimes the system is the system."

Three months into his recovery, Scott was still getting special duty pay, as though he were still jumping out of airplanes and SCUBA diving. He laughed when he remembered the Air Force clarifying his status: "Eventually, the system caught up to me and wanted to take it all back at once. All of a sudden, I had zero pay but I still needed to put food on the table."

Scott got a part-time job selling the *Encyclopaedia Britannica*. Scott would set up a booth in a local mall or connect with potential customers through local community facilities. "I had to talk even though I still had a tube in my throat," he said. "Every time I wanted to say something, I had to cover the end of the tube and force the air in my lungs out past that hole and over my vocal cords. I got plenty of weird looks."

Scott says that he felt neither anger nor the desire to blame anyone for the circumstances in which he found himself. He just wanted to get better.

During the summer of 1987, less than six months after the accident, the personnel center of the Air Force caught up with Scott and offered him a medical retirement. He declined it. "I wanted to retrain as a pararescue and be a PJ again," he said. "I was alive. I had a lot to look forward to."

Scott was given the opportunity to cross-train, but he didn't want that either. "The Air Force is responsible for healing you as much as you can be healed," he explained. "They said my current career field was no longer possible, since I still had a two-inch tube sticking out of my throat, so my job was over unless I wanted to go be a trainer in a gym or something. But I didn't want to do that. Three weeks later they called me back to say they were going to take away my Air Force specialty code and classify me as an airman awaiting retraining." Scott still wanted to retrain as a pararescueman and be a PJ.

Scott was making progress, but it was relative. "I was unable to eat solid food, and since all I had done was lie in a hospital bed, I had gotten so skinny I looked like a prisoner of war," he told me. "I hadn't been able to move much in the hospital, so my muscles atrophied and of course my jaw was wired shut," he said. "There was a McDonald's in the hospital that drove me crazy because I could smell it. All I wanted was to eat a french fry! I used to try to wedge a Popsicle stick between my teeth and try to turn it in a vertical position just so that I might open my mouth a quarter of an inch and bite a single french fry. I couldn't do it!"

What he could do was to force one of those french fries between his teeth and into his mouth. But even that did not help him achieve his goal. Unable to chew it, he nearly choked trying to swallow it.

The Air Force flight surgeon offered Scott a medical discharge—again. Scott looked him straight in the eye and said, "I want to continue doing my job as a pararescueman. I want to recover and at least have the opportunity to be a PJ again."

The surgeon paused, then said, "It's on you."

"I was thirty at the time of the accident," Scott said, "and I turned thirty-one while I was recovering. I still had my whole life in front of me and pararescue was the only work I wanted to do."

Scott had been a fit 185 pounds at the time of the accident, a regular runner, biker, and swimmer. After his ordeal, he was an emaciated 150 pounds. "As bad as it was, I wasn't depressed or discouraged," he said. "My confidence was connected to a sense of being in good hands, I think, with my doctors."

Rebuilding his fitness proved to be a slow process, but Scott was lucky. He hadn't damaged his spinal cord. He could walk, he could exercise, and eventually he started running. Progress came in tiny increments, but it came: "I would do one push-up, then two, and then ten. I just kept pushing," he said.

"People have a choice, you know? I know I could have left. I made a choice to stay. I made a choice to be alive. That informed everything I did after the accident."

The multiple surgeries had left Scott with an area of inflammation called a granuloma: scar tissue formed where he had received the initial cricothyroidotomy on the day of the accident. As the scar tissue thickened, it blocked Scott's throat and made it difficult for him to breathe.

Scott didn't want to tell anyone about the complication because he was afraid that he would be sent back to the hospital or deterred from his goal of returning to active duty. But eventually he found it so difficult to breathe that he could not sleep, and he sought medical care.

A cycle commenced where doctors removed scar tissue from Scott's throat, which gave him a few weeks of relief before the tissue regenerated and Scott was suffocating again. Then the doctors repeated the procedure.

"Like Nails Hitting Your Face"

The scar tissue grew back so quickly that Scott's medical team concluded that he needed a tracheotomy, an incision into the windpipe. This procedure restored Scott's ability to breathe, but left him with a tube sticking out of his neck that he had to cover every time he wanted to talk.

Over the following eight months, Scott underwent nine laser surgeries on the granuloma. Between the surgeries, he ran and lifted weights and hoped that his throat could be fixed. It was more than an annoyance. It was a potential career buster.

"I couldn't swim because of that tube," he said. "I never lost sight of my goal to become a PJ again, and I needed to swim, but I couldn't do that while I had the hole in my throat." Training includes an extensive swimming component because the underwater needs on the job can be high. Many pararescue candidates drop out during the swimming phase of the training.

"The training is intense because there is no room for error on this job," Scott said.

"Imagine doing a water rescue with helos hovering over you with their rotors spinning," Scott said. "It's like you're in a hurricane, and the water can feel like nails hitting your face."

In early 1988, Scott was still an airman awaiting retraining, living his life while breathing through a tube in his throat and looking for a better solution. He finally found one from a former member of the Marine Corps Reserve who was working in Boston as a surgeon. Dr. William Montgomery, who had invented flexible tracheotomy tubes, told Scott that his trachea was about the size of the eraser on a pencil.

"That is the size of a baby's trachea," Montgomery told him. "It's no wonder you can't breathe."

Over the course of two surgeries, Montgomery reconstructed Scott's trachea. By August 1988, Scott was finally able to get rid of the breathing tube permanently—and swim again. Two months later, he was ready to take the physical training (PT) test.

In order to be returned to flight status, Scott needed to pass a physical test at Fort Bragg, North Carolina, and he needed to obtain a waiver from the surgeon general of the Air Force. Scott had been training hard, and he knew he was going to pass that PT test, a series of timed runs and swims. "In the end, I didn't struggle a whole lot with that," he said, shrugging at the thought.

But Scott was worried that his head injury and the amount of time he had been unconscious after the fall were going to make it hard for him to get the medical waiver. The amount of time that Scott spent unconscious after the fall was never fully determined, which made it tricky to predict how the doctors would feel about restoring his flight status. Scott felt like he needed a miracle to get his job back.

There is usually a space on military medical forms where you are supposed to describe your health. When Scott was filling out his forms for the waiver and got to this space, it would have been standard for him to write something like, "My health is excellent."

Scott wrote, "My health is excellent. I run a seven-minute mile. Can you?" He had done everything in his power to get his job back. Now his future was in someone else's hands.

"I got a phone call from my doctor a couple of weeks later

to say that the paperwork was back, and could I come down and discuss it," he said. "I was so anxious as I headed down there. He handed me a sheaf of papers, and all that I saw was this note from the doctor under my cocky answer about the seven-minute mile. The doctor had written, 'Maybe, but I can answer the whole question. What about medications?'"

At that point, Scott recalled, "I thought it was over, that I was done for. But then I looked at the second page and I saw that big stamp of approval, 'Medically Acceptable.'"

Scott was a PJ again.

Another Jump, Another Malfunction

Two weeks later, and eighteen months after the accident, Scott did his ninety-first free fall. Once again, there was a malfunction. "We jumped out of a C-130 over the Gulf of Mexico at 13,000 feet and planned to open our parachutes at 3,500 feet, but after I pulled the ripcord handle I did not feel the normal opening shock of the parachute, and I knew something was wrong," he told me.

"I looked over my shoulder and my parachute was trailing out of the pack. I went through the emergency procedures in my head. I knew I had between five and ten seconds to make a choice. As I was shaking the risers, trying to help the parachute to open, I remember thinking, 'I can't believe this is happening. I might be having another bad landing.'"

At 2,700 feet, Scott knew he needed to go to his emergency handle, but just as he reached for the reserve parachute, his primary parachute opened after all. That jump was a water jump and officials determined later that the parachutes they had been using for water jumps were not opening properly because the material would stick together and briefly resist coming apart after opening. These particular canopies were eventually taken out of service.

Over the course of his career, Scott did a total of about five hundred free falls and static falls before he was finally medically retired—after twenty-two years of service. He still deals with pain from the injury and other smaller injuries he incurred over the years.

"I wouldn't go to the flight surgeon unless I really couldn't stand it, because I didn't want to be grounded, to be off status waiting to be healed," he said.

Scott believes that PJs understand the risks of their position, and he has no regrets. "You're going to get banged up on this job," he said. "If someone gets through a tour as a pararescueman without any injuries, he was either very lucky or else he never left his desk!"

Soon after Scott returned to work as a PJ, he accepted an assignment as an instructor at the Pararescue School at Kirtland Air Force Base in Texas, where he volunteered to instruct the Civil Air Patrol Pararescue Orientation Course, called PJOC, for teenagers. The Civil Air Patrol is an organization of civilians interested in aviation who volunteer to act as an auxiliary to the Air Force in emergency situations and who provide assistance to other agencies and organizations, like local police, when needed. PJOC is still run by active-duty PJs who instruct young cadets who might someday join the Air Force and try to become PJs themselves. It was while Scott was teaching this course, on August 2, 1990, that Iraq invaded Kuwait.

"I knew they were going to need combat search and rescue and I wanted to be there," he said. But as an instructor in a training unit, he was not on an operational team.

When he got back from Kirtland, Scott drew up a list of volunteers from his unit who were willing to go into the combat zone. Three months later, Scott was on his way to Southwest Asia as a volunteer for Desert Storm. He deployed to Saudi Arabia to the 1723rd Special Tactics Squadron and was asked to lead the combat search and rescue team.

At the forward operating base, Scott came across Major Corby Martin, an MH-53 helicopter pilot who had been a lieutenant when they were both stationed at Royal Air Force Woodbridge in England. While assigning PJs to helicopter crews, Corby told Scott he wanted Scott to join him on his crew. Scott didn't know it at the time, but Corby had been a lead planner for Eager Anvil, the mission that kicked off Desert Storm.

The plan was to fly fast and low at night, over desert terrain, and lead a group of Army Apache helicopters to neutralize the Iraqi air-defense system.

When you are part of a crew like that, everyone is responsible for calling out anything they might see. That night, Scott saw light coming out of the darkness. At first, he thought he was seeing a motorcycle headlight, but Scott quickly realized that it was a missile coming toward them, and he called it out by clock position.

The pilot made an evasive maneuver and they all avoided certain death. They made it to their objective, the mission was successful, and a gigantic hole was opened in the Iraqi air defense, allowing US and Allied forces to enter. "There were so many aircraft in the air it looked like the sky was flowing in the opposite direction that night," Scott said. If Scott had not worked so hard to be a PJ again, he would have missed this important battle.

Search and Rescue behind Enemy Lines

In January 1991, PJs under Scott's leadership as the noncommissioned officer in charge rescued Navy pilot Devon Jones a day after his F-14 was shot down over Baghdad. It was the first combat search and rescue behind enemy lines since Vietnam.

When Scott returned from Desert Storm, he was selected to be the first Air Force instructor at the Army Special Forces Underwater Operations School, or SCUBA school, in Key West, Florida.

"It was a rough assignment, but somebody had to do it," he joked. After three years of teaching, Scott became restless and took a position on the special tactics team in England.

Over the next four years, he led the team in rotations in Southern Italy made necessary by the conflicts in Yugoslavia, Bosnia and Herzegovina, and Serbia. During the Serbian conflict, Scott's team needed personnel from other units. One of these pararescuemen, Jeremy Hardy, had been in Scott's Civil Air Patrol Pararescue Orientation Course ten years earlier, when Jeremy was fourteen.

Jeremy credited Scott with inspiring him then to become a PJ. That meant a lot to Scott. "You just never know when or where or how you might influence someone," he said.

Scott was medically retired in 2002. "I tried to stay in, but this time the system really caught up with me," he said. Scott experienced many injuries, aches, and pains during his career that he was often reluctant to bring to anyone's attention for fear of missing a mission. "You don't want to be categorized as DNIF [does not include flying] for a common cold or a sprain," he said. "I sucked up injuries my whole career."

In 2002, Scott experienced a more intense version of what he had come to consider "normal" back pain. When he finally saw a flight surgeon, he was told that he had been walking around with four slipped discs and four herniated discs, and that about a third of his vertebrae were broken and had slid out of alignment. Scott was grounded, and that started the process of his medical retirement.

Scott went on to provide security as a contractor at the US Embassy in Baghdad and at a gold mine in Indonesia. He has also worked for the Department of Homeland Security.

"I've done a lot of exciting things since I left active duty, but I would enlist in the Air Force again today if I could," he said.

Most servicemen are familiar with DD Form 214, the Certificate of Release or Discharge from Active Duty. "The last line on that form says I could be recalled at any time to active duty, and every time I read it, I think, what the hell are they waiting for?" he said.

He recalled his job as a PJ "the adventure of a lifetime."

"The things we got to do, the friendships and bonds I built with my teammates. I'm guessing that a normal civilian job does not provide that. When you fly with a helicopter crew, you build something with the entire crew. You may all die together. When you are out there on the line, you are in the fight for your life and for the life of the person next to you."

I know what he means and I understand the powerful draw of that brotherhood. Scott credits that brotherhood for much of his success. "I have always been part of a team," Scott said. "Early in my life, it was baseball and football; later in my career, I was part of a special forces team, a SEAL team, the Air Force team, and of course, my family. I played a part in my own recovery, but I couldn't have done it without my family or my team."

HEROES GIVE AND GET HELP

Scott is humble and matter-of-fact about the sheer grit he has displayed over many years, but he is lavish with his praise for the people who have played a role in his recovery and career. When I follow his lead and think about myself as a member of a team, and remain conscious that my choices will affect other people in ways that I might not anticipate, I consider the larger implications of my own conduct and the conduct of the people with whom I work.

Scott projects a remarkable sense of calm. I'm betting that his attitude comes from living a life fully in sync with his values and goals. "Everyone is going to have good days and bad days," Scott said. "But no matter how bleak your future may look, don't quit. You have got to dig deep and find something that motivates you. You don't know what you are capable of until you break the boundaries you think you have around you."

I am humbled by Scott's tenacity and perseverance in fighting to put himself back on the line by becoming a PJ again after such an enormous accident. Remember that PJs are responsible for rescue and recovery. There are sailors, Marines, airmen, and soldiers who get into situations where they go above and beyond and save the day, but that is the job—day in and day out—of pararescuemen.

No one would have faulted Scott for taking a medical retirement or a less taxing job after his fall. But Scott wanted to be a PJ again—and he made it happen. "I thought it was the greatest job in the world; I did it because I loved it," Scott said. "And the funny thing is that most people don't know that the Air Force has this job at all."

When I am deploying, I need to trust that my brothers and sisters downrange have my back. I want the people I work with to know that they can count on me, so I don't want to do anything that would make them find me untrustworthy. That requires a commitment of loyalty in my private conduct as well as in my public conduct.

For example, fraternization is occasionally a problem in the military, just as it is in many other workplaces. One of the many reasons that fraternization needs to be discouraged is that it can destroy loyalty within a unit. Fraternization breeds distrust. I don't ever want to question whether someone has my back, or whether someone in my squad, my platoon, or even my company has met the standards they need to meet in order to do their job. If someone is in an inappropriate workplace relationship, they are giving me reason to doubt their integrity and their qualifications. That will interfere with the loyalty team members need to have in order to be successful.

Balancing Competing Loyalties

Sometimes people get confused about competing loyalties, especially in the military. When soldiers begin to serve, they might think that the unit comes first and family comes second. That is what I thought. I was wrong.

It is challenging but possible—and important—to strike a balance between job and family. It can be difficult to strike that balance. In a firefight, of course, the unit is most important in that moment. When a unit is training to go overseas, that unit is often more important day to day.

When I was overseas, I sometimes found it hard to maintain contact with my family. Early on, I was often working for more than twelve hours at a stretch without access to a phone. But it was my responsibility to be in touch with my family. When my training was over and my deployment was done, I was going home to my family.

I don't think that I have always done my best to let my family know how important they are to me. That was especially true when I was younger. Even though I relied on my brothers in combat, when everything was over we all returned home to our loved ones. Those of us who had not been cultivating our relationships at home often did not find the support we needed there. As a result, we were not as strong when we subsequently returned to our units.

Shared experiences can promote loyalty, especially when the experiences are intense. In the Ranger unit, struggling together built loyalty. My loyalty to the 75th Ranger Regiment grew stronger as I went through the daily routines of training. The effort required to meet expectations as a Ranger, or a SEAL, or a PJ is enormous, and as I put in the effort to meet those expectations, I identified more strongly as a Ranger.

Training to become a Ranger is brutal. I was in good shape when I got into the Army, but if the physical challenge and discipline required even in basic training were a swift kick in the nuts, then the Ranger Indoctrination Program was a full beatdown.

My natural athletic ability combined with the training I had undergone for football through college had given me a good fitness base, but the physical demands of Ranger Indoctrination were more punishing than anything I had experienced before.

The pressure that we were all under to pass, just to remain in the class, built loyalty within the squad because we were all suffering together. I developed loyalty to the 75th Ranger Regiment because I was inspired by the challenges put in front of me. I was pushed to my limits, but as I met the expectations and survived to train another day, my loyalty to the regiment and to my brothers grew stronger.

"If You Step Out, You're Done!"

We were sweating and training together and depending on each other to get each other through. Each one of us had things we struggled with, and everyone had a bad day here and there. I remember doing ruck marches during the infantry courses and watching guys fall out. Most days, I could carry two rucksacks and still keep up, so if a guy was starting to fall out, I would take his ruck, and literally lighten his load so that he could keep moving.

Someone did that for me during my final march in the Florida phase of Ranger School. I had been pushing the limits of my endurance for weeks by the time we got to the end of the Florida phase. I had been given an extra sleeping bag to carry on this particular ruck march, and I had bungeed it into a ball on the top of my ruck.

The addition to my pack didn't make it any heavier, but it also didn't allow my machine gun to settle properly. My shoulder began to hurt as soon as I started moving. After about six miles, I started to fall back. We still had six or seven miles to go. My shoulder was killing me, and the pain was radiating into my lower back. I stepped out of line to try to adjust the backpack, but the Ranger instructor noticed right away and shouted at me to fall back in: "If you step out, you're done!"

I remember thinking, "I can't believe this is happening." The idea that I might not make it, that I might not graduate, with only seven miles left in my entire Ranger School experience, seemed impossible, since up until that night I had always found being able to carry heavy rucks easier than most, but not on this night. At that moment, an Infantry Officer Basic Course guy approached me and said, "Paronto, give me the machine gun."

He was not a particularly strong guy, and I had actually helped him several times over the previous few weeks. I was relieved, but also embarrassed, to have our positions reversed. "You've been helping me this whole way," he told me, and held out his hand to take my weapon. I handed it over and took his much lighter M4 carbine in exchange.

I finished the march, and credit that achievement to my lightened load and the grace that came from having received help in my moment of need. That exchange happened because the members of our unit had developed loyalty by sharing daily routines and experiences, and by helping each other to complete group tasks.

Teamwork builds loyalty. When there is a common mission, one person can't do everything, so you depend on each other to accomplish tasks. During basic training, we used to have marksmanship competitions, where our group would do dry-fire drills—in which live ammunition is not used. In that case, I wanted to come out on top because the whole team had to shoot well and I didn't want to let anyone down.

Leaders can also inspire loyalty. Some of my instructors

were veterans from Somalia, and even if I didn't always know the details of what they had done, I knew where they had been and a little bit of what they had survived. When these veterans were preparing us to be Rangers, they were sometimes harsh, but I respected their judgment and their wisdom. I understood why they were making us suffer. We knew we would each need to depend on the guy next to us. I have a better chance of surviving on the battlefield if I do all I can to make sure the guy next to me survives, because we protect each other.

I will always be loyal to the Ranger Battalion. When bad things happen downrange, I know that I can talk to my brothers, and I know that we can pump each other up or rally around each other in times of need. But as I have gotten older, I have begun to pay more attention to the way I demonstrate loyalty to my family.

Learning to Cherish Family

I don't know that anyone in the Army ever told me to put my unit before my loved ones, but I absorbed that message and became caught up in the intensity and immediacy of my Ranger responsibilities at the expense of my responsibilities to my family.

Over the years, I have come to understand that the rock of my family on which I rely creates a positive energy that fuels me. The support of my family is what has allowed me to deploy again. When I have been lost, my loved ones are the people who have helped me find my way.

I called Tanya, my wife, as soon as I had access to a telephone after our fight in Benghazi ended. I wanted to tell her I was okay and I wanted to tell her what had happened.

My wife was my first call in less dramatic circumstances,

too. In 2006, I had volunteered to do a surveillance walk in Kabul late at night. I was disguised as a local government worker, walking around on my own. On these kinds of jobs, we were tasked with doing surveillance on specific apartments, or locating particular people or vehicles in order to verify information from our assets, or getting a general lay of the land.

This assignment was in a neighborhood that was dangerous not just because of the potential Taliban activity but because of ordinary crime. The plan was for me to get dropped off in one spot and then walk a few miles in and out of particular blocks and buildings before getting picked up at another point.

The tricky thing about this operation was that I wouldn't have the standard kind of backup we like to have. Placing a full team nearby would have been so conspicuous that it would have compromised the whole operation.

Instead, I had one guy—named Popeye—who was supposed to be circling the area in a vehicle. If I needed rescuing, Popeye might be coming from five minutes away. Five minutes may not sound like much time, but it can be an eternity if you are in trouble.

Dressed like a government worker in trousers and a suit jacket, I was dropped off at dusk. I was carrying a concealed Glock 19 pistol but no body armor. This was early in my career, and I remember feeling nervous as I walked along those narrow streets in the twilight. I could feel adrenaline racing through my body, and I felt as though all of my senses were amplified. You could call it paranoia. As I moved through the neighborhood checking things off, I was acutely conscious of how long it would take for backup to get to me if something went wrong, so I walked as quickly as I could without calling attention to myself, but still trying to efficiently complete my surveillance of the area.

When I got the information we needed and made it to the pickup location without an incident, I discovered that everyone on my team was waiting and full of questions, asking me what I saw and strategizing about how to put the intelligence to use. I was amped up and wanted to talk about it, but the person I really wanted to tell was Tanya. I called her as soon as I got back to the base and told her as much as I could without compromising OPSEC (operational security). When I think about that now, I am motivated to continue to work harder to balance my loyalties to all of my teams and live in a way that reflects my values.

EMBRACING THE VALUES
LOYALTY

We are each part of a larger team or series of teams. We are each responsible for cultivating the self-awareness and the honesty needed to assess accurately our own character. Part of being honest with yourself requires clarifying your own values. Loyalty is at the core of any well-functioning unit. I feel loyal to my family, to the members of my units, and to the United States and its Constitution, which I have vowed to protect and defend.

You have to ask yourself: If I don't feel loyalty to this unit, what am I doing in this unit? Why am I a part of this organization? Why am I a part of this family? Why am I in this marriage?

Those are some heavy questions. Answering these questions will require clarifying your goals and values. If your loyalty is truly not there for any particular relationship, then you shouldn't be there. If you do want to be there, you need to figure out how to locate and display your loyalty. Either way, you need to fix yourself.

Being loyal means carrying out your responsibilities and accomplishing your assigned tasks—even if, at that particular moment, you dislike your leaders and your unit. That also holds true for members of your household and your coworkers. You can display your loyalty by committing to accomplishing your mission, even if you don't have the tools you need. When you are someone whom others can trust and depend on, you are living loyalty.

A lack of loyalty will destroy a unit or a department or a family, because mistrust will develop and the unit's cohesion will weaken. In my line of work, you are there to serve your country. If you are not loyal to the United States and don't have a vested interest in your brothers and sisters in arms, you will not give fully of yourself. You may be in a situation where you have to put the interests of your unit, or your country, ahead of your own. If you don't feel that bone-deep loyalty, you may not do it.

Team America!

What if we started thinking about the United States, all the people of America, as one team? What if we all operated as though we each had something to contribute? What if we had a mutual commitment to our team, as leaders, and as those being led? I think our country would look pretty different.

I'm not arguing for blind loyalty. True loyalty requires speaking up if you think something is wrong. Everyone makes mistakes. Everyone makes bad calls.

You can't be a good soldier without obeying your leaders; you have no choice in the matter. But soldiers are not supposed to obey unlawful orders, which underscores the point that no one man or leader is higher than the Constitution.

Unfortunately, sometimes you find a leader who lacks the moral integrity to stand up for his or her troops if a decision is made that might threaten the mission.

Sometimes you find leaders who refuse to yield on principle when circumstances mandate that they yield. This will then force a soldier to fall back on other core values, such as duty. Being able to identify and resist injustice within a unit will lead to a stronger overall organization. Bad leadership can occur in any organization, from a family to a police department to the military. You can demonstrate your loyalty by calling out bad leadership when you see it.

Loyalty keeps you connected to people who care about you. Those people are often your family members, but they don't need to be related to you. Whoever they are, you need those people in order to be your best self. You cannot be a lone wolf in the military and you cannot generally be a lone wolf in life. You may lose the support of your loved ones if you are disloyal, and then you will become vulnerable to people who may not have your best interests at heart.

CHAPTER FOUR

DUTY

Fulfill your obligations. Doing your duty means more than carrying out your assigned tasks. Duty means being able to accomplish tasks as part of a team. The work of the U.S. Army is a complex combination of missions, tasks and responsibilities— all in constant motion. Our work entails building one assignment onto another. You fulfill your obligations as a part of your unit every time you resist the temptation to take "shortcuts" that might undermine the integrity of the final product.

BELIEVE IT IS MY DUTY to be the best person I can be: morally, ethically, physically, emotionally. I'm far from perfect, and I don't expect to ever stop making mistakes, but it is my duty to try to do my best in all of those areas.

A team is only as strong as its weakest link. If any team members take shortcuts or fail to fulfill their responsibilities, they will increase the possibility that a team mission will fail.

It is like a dam with a weak spot: eventually, that dam could break at that vulnerable place if it doesn't get fixed. People often won't notice small, weak spots, or they might see them but not address them. That is a risk.

It is important to identify members of your team who have substandard training or skills, or who are lacking in integrity, and to figure out how to address those issues. On the individual level, it's important to keep identifying and working on patching up our own weak spots. Life is in constant motion. The best plans can change in an instant. When everyone is routinely fulfilling their duties and maintaining their responsibilities to the group, then the team is always ready to pivot, adapt, and respond if the mission needs to change.

When the shit hits the fan, everyone needs to be a team player, not a me player. Otherwise, the likelihood that the mission will fail increases. In my line of work, when a mission fails, people may die. I am thinking not only of my own teammates, but also of innocent bystanders or other first responders.

If a member of my team is not trained properly, or doesn't have good judgment, that person may take a bad shot. I've said before that I have to be able to trust that my team has my back, and that everyone is willing to put their life on the line. But I also need to count on my teammates to know what they are doing in more mundane circumstances, to know that they will do their duty and respond correctly in any situation.

Rangers are forced to work as a team right from the start. When they sent trucks to pick us up to take us to Ranger Battalion for the first time, they told us we had to put all of our bags on the back of one of the trucks in no more than thirty seconds. We had to scramble as a group to make that happen, but managed to get our bags neatly stacked and loaded in about thirty seconds.

The Ranger instructor seemed surprised, and since the whole purpose of the task was to have an excuse to show us what happens when you come up short, they played a little mind-fuck game with us, telling us we must be idiots because we put everything on the wrong truck. We had twenty seconds to move all the gear to a second truck. We had to work together to succeed and we were going to be punished together if we failed. Hell, we were going to be punished together either way.

No Shortcuts in Ranger School

We couldn't ever take shortcuts in Ranger School. Guys who were generally meeting standards might get a second chance at retraining on a particular skill they were having trouble with. For example, an otherwise competent candidate may be given the opportunity to re-test, once, on the task she or he failed, but ultimately they need to meet the standard. Everyone really did have to pass everything. Airborne School was not as intense as Ranger School, but there were no shortcuts there either, because if we messed up on the job, we were increasing our odds of dying or killing someone else.

At Ranger Battalion, every mission had to be coordinated down to the last individual. Let's say that a unit is assigned to carry out a direct-action mission in a village. The fire teams that will move through the village to clear the houses will have to coordinate with the machine-gun teams on the hill. Failure to do so could mean they risk being shot by their own guys.

As a machine gunner, I would be watching for signals from the fire teams. A red signal flare means that the fire team is stuck in one building and can't move forward. A green signal flare means that the fire team has cleared the house it was in and is moving to the next spot. That means that the machine guns need to shift fire to another target or set of targets. Teamwork is essential, because if you don't work together, even in a training situation, someone may die who should not have.

I remember the Army built a mock village at Yakima

Training Center in Washington, where I had one of my first training ops. The military created Special Ops Command several years after the infamous failure in 1980 of Operation Eagle Claw, the aborted attempt to rescue the fifty-two US Embassy staff being held captive at the embassy in Tehran. Eight servicemen were killed. The military analyzed the fiasco and issued a report recommending areas of improvement across different branches. By the time I got there, air and ground elements were coordinating and training together. We had an Air Force element, an AC-130 Spectre gunship, and we also had little birds called Night Stalkers from the 160th Special Operations Aviation Regiment (SOAR) providing air support as well as transporting Rangers to fast rope into the objective. The 160th SOAR is the elite helicopter team out of Fort Campbell, Kentucky, that supports all special ops branches of service.

Low Man on the Totem Pole

I had not yet attended Ranger School, so I was the lowest guy on the totem pole, an untabbed private. My job was to be an ammo bearer, which meant that I was holding extra ammunition for the machine guns. I remember sitting in on the briefing, watching and listening and being grateful that I was not in charge. There were so many elements to this plan of attack, I wouldn't have known where to begin. We had a three-dimensional model of the mock village (we called it the sandtable), and the leaders were using it to walk us through the plan: they would point and say, "This is where helo X is going to land and Squad A is going to be on helo Y over here" and so on. It was important to be clear, because when all of the helicopters started flying, one could crash into another if any one of them was off even a little bit. It was going to be chaos out there, and it would be even worse in the dark.

We had to rely on the 160th SOAR to get where we needed to go. Once we dropped down, we needed to move a little bit. At this point, my M240G machine-gun team was supposed to be up on a hill along with the Carl Gustaf Recoilless–rifle teams, putting suppressive fire into the mock villages so that the fire teams could begin assaulting the objectives. Our task was to fire from a distance in and around Building One where the bad guys would be, and then shift to Building Two when the line squads alerted us via green star clusters (a flare) that they were ready to actually physically enter into Building One to either apprehend a high-value target or surgically clear the area, depending on the objective. This would happen continuously until all buildings were cleared and the objective was secure.

Completing such an operation successfully requires an amazing amount of precision, coordination, and teamwork. There are little birds—helicopters—doing strafing runs while the Ranger squads are landing and moving to assault the objective. The little birds are flying low and raining down hate with their 2.75 rockets and miniguns, and blowing things up so everything is already getting peppered as the guys on the ground start moving.

When the birds are low, they are all you can hear when you are standing on the ground. The guys in the birds will be on standby so that if the machine-gun teams aren't getting everything, the birds can come in and provide some suppressive power. Let's say that a fire team is crossing over a fence and through a front yard on their way to a house that they need to clear. The machine-gun team is shooting into that house as the fire team runs toward the house. When the fire team shoots a green flare into the sky, the machine-gun team knows it's time to redirect its fire to the next house. At the same time, the fire team runs into the house that had been getting torn up by machine-gun fire.

I am describing a training exercise, so in some ways, it's not real. But in other ways, it is, since the exercise uses live fire. We were shooting real bullets and real rockets and using real miniguns. We had a Spectre above us that needed to fire a little farther because it was suppressing a different area. I could hear the buzz of the Spectre gun, the hammer of the miniguns, and the pop of the 102 howitzer cannon all around me, but I couldn't see any of them until they hit and I could see the explosions.

We had machine-gun fire, flares going up, and little birds doing their strafing runs when the C-130 Spectre hit. There were constant explosions in my night-vision goggles. Most of us were just learning this stuff.

How was it possible that no one was dying? Because of the intense teamwork, coordination, and commitment to duty. Nobody had an ego and nobody was putting himself above the team. Some guys might have been arrogant, but everyone knew his job and exactly what he was supposed to do and when he was supposed to do it. Our leaders were clear about what they needed from each of us, and we were each clear about our particular duty to the mission.

Teamwork was essential for us to accomplish this complicated mission in the middle of chaos, and a sense of duty was essential to creating a successful team. In the Army, the machine is what succeeds, not any individual soldier. The

Rangers succeed, not Ranger Paronto. A person does not belong in the military if he or she can't handle that. But a person does not have to be in the military to fulfill obligations and provide a great service to a team.

Values That Work in the Army Work in Civilian Life, Too

Duty is a key value at work, even if your life isn't on the line. When I was in graduate school, I took a job at Mutual of Omaha as an insurance adjuster. My goal, at that time, was to get back into the military, so I wasn't working in the job of my dreams, but I understood that I had a duty to do good work and to accomplish the goals that were set for me.

We had teams of half a dozen people assigned to accomplish particular goals. The goal might have been to process a certain number of insurance adjustment files by a particular deadline, so it wasn't a life-or-death situation. But our team had to work together to meet the deadline, and if any one of us didn't carry his or her weight, our whole team would be reprimanded, and there were consequences for the people waiting on those claims.

I discovered that, as I had seen in the military, shared goals and positive attitudes made our team fire on all cylinders. I worked as fast as I could because I didn't want our mission to fail and I didn't want to lose a bonus. But I also really didn't want to let my team down. The stakes were different, but the value of the teamwork we displayed was just as important.

When I started at Omaha, I had two great bosses—Scott Holmes, a former Air Force JAG officer, and Jerry Dubyak, a Vietnam veteran Air Force pilot. I do not think it was a coincidence that both of these men turned out to be excellent commanders as civilians. Scott and Jerry knew how to get things done, and they knew how to command without yelling or creating dissent.

We all learned the same methods for investigating fraud and reviewing files, and that helped us get things done harmoniously. Scott and Jerry created strong team environments with integrity, they made work fun, and they helped the people who worked there train with consistent processes. I'm still in touch with guys from that job.

ROB JABER

Rob Jaber is another guy with whom I worked and still keep in touch. Rob went through a training course at Blackwater, the American private military company, with Dave Benton and me, and I liked him right away. Most of the guys in contractor trainings are former military men. Rob had no military background, but he held his own among the special ops guys.

Some of the former military guys wanted to make sure everyone in the training environment understood who they were, and I can imagine someone in Rob's position being intimidated, but he was not. Instead, Rob projected a quiet confidence in his own skills and abilities, and he quickly earned my respect.

Rob, who lived in Lebanon as a child, could also speak Arabic. In the early 1980s, as war was breaking out in Lebanon, Rob's father secured permanent visas for his family to come to the United States. Rob and his siblings learned and spoke English at schools in Michigan, but the Jaber family continued to speak Arabic at home.

In 1993, Rob graduated from high school and, six years

later, graduated from the University of Michigan–Dearborn with a major in economics and a minor in business.

Rob worked as a management trainee at a bank and moved on to several jobs like that until he was working at Morgan Stanley as a financial advisor. To an observer, it must have seemed like Rob was on a straight path, advancing in his career and taking on volunteer work in the local business community in organizations like the Chamber of Commerce.

But even as he was succeeding, Rob was discovering that he didn't want to work behind a desk. In his free time, Rob began training to be a reserve officer with the Wayne County Sheriff's Office, and he found that the active way of life it required was one he wanted to pursue professionally.

Rob's fluency in Arabic was his ticket. Rob accepted a six-month contract in Iraq with an organization called WorldWide Language Resources in 2003. "I thought I'd do it for the heck of it," he said. "Six months seemed like a good length of time to try. I asked my uncle if he wanted to do it, too, and he said yes, so we went over together and both worked as translators."

It would be Rob's first time being away from family and friends.

At first, Rob was assigned to assist a military unit that took money from the airport in Baghdad to the Central Bank of Iraq. Rob blended in, as long as he didn't speak. "As soon as I spoke, locals could tell from my dialect that I was different," he said. "On the other hand, people didn't always assume Americans could understand them, and sometimes if there were personnel around with their own interpreters, I would pretend that I couldn't understand and be able to do a bit of a double check."

Toward the end of that contract, Rob was attached to the Defense Intelligence Agency. His new team "ran sources and tried to collect high-value intelligence," he said. "This was less routine work than I had been doing, and it was pretty interesting. I started to meet other guys working on the premiere detail and got exposed to other security contracting opportunities."

At the end of the contract, Rob returned home to Michigan and began training to work as a protective security specialist for Blackwater. That's when I met him, and we both deployed right afterward. Rob remembers feeling more comfortable in Iraq when he returned: "I knew what I was getting into. I knew some locals; I had made some contacts during my first assignment. I was able to drive because I already knew a lot of the roads. Most of the people working in Baghdad then lived in the same protected, general area, so I knew a lot of those guys, too." Rob's uncle was also still in Baghdad, working for Rob's former company on a new contract.

"Odd Man Out"

Even though this was Rob's second trip to Iraq, and he felt more sure of himself, he was still feeling his way in his new role. "It was different really being a member of a security team," he said. "My background was different. I felt like I was the odd man out. Most of the other guys had time in the military, and longevity, and specialties under their belts that I didn't. I was a little unsure of myself and worried that I was underqualified."

Rob had to remind himself that he had passed the training course and that he belonged there like everyone else. I was surprised when Rob later told me how unsure he felt at the time, because he was assigned to my team and I remember him always having a great attitude, like, "Let's do this job and get it going." When I told him that, he said, "Well, I loved it. Even though I had my moments of doubt, I liked what I was doing so much better than when I had been working a desk job!"

Rob's status as the unit's sole Muslim and the only person of Arabic descent made him feel self-conscious. "We were in the Middle East so we would hear the calls to prayer during the day, and sometimes someone would make a disparaging comment," he said.

Each time that happened, Rob spoke up. "I'd say something like, 'I'm standing next to you. I don't disrespect your religion; don't disrespect mine.'"

Rob, who had attended Catholic schools, grew up respecting other religions. "Most of the guys were great, and I felt like we were brothers," he said of the unit. "We were living together, six hundred guys in these boxes in the desert, almost like shipping containers cut in half, where they made rooms. You bet we got to know each other. We might think differently, we might have different outlooks on different topics, but at the end of the day we came together and we trusted each other. I knew that if the shit hit the fan, they would have my back."

Rob's language skills made him invaluable. "We were tasked with making things more secure, and we always got what we wanted done," he said, "often because, I think, I was able to be more nuanced when we talked with people. Many locals were a little more cooperative with me, and I didn't have to worry about whether an interpreter was translating properly."

Rob enjoyed the work and re-upped his contracts, which normally ran three months on and one month off, through 2009. "We always joked around about how many close calls we had had," Rob said. "'I've got four more to go on my nine lives,' that kind of joking."

Rob had married in 2008, and he and his wife started a family right away. "I always saw contracting as an opportunity, not a career," he said. "I promised my wife that I would do one more contract after the one I was on expired and that I would come home by the end of the year and call it quits in 2010, no matter what."

Rob hoped his next career move would be in law enforcement or the civil service, and he applied for jobs with the FBI, the Secret Service, and the Federal Air Marshal Service.

"I had applied for those jobs before," he said, "and I would get these generic emails saying there was no hiring in my area. Once I started working with people downrange while I was contracting, I made some helpful contacts and felt like I was making progress."

Rob started undergoing the extensive testing required by some of these organizations. He would schedule those tests during his time off, when he was home, and he began passing the written tests, panel interviews, and physical training tests, and started to feel optimistic about his possibilities for life after contracting. "I didn't feel exactly politically motivated," he told me, "but I felt like I was doing a meaningful job, helping to keep Americans safe. I felt like I was acting for the people, for our people, and I wanted to make it my career."

I enjoyed working with Rob overseas. Some interpreters don't carry weapons, but Rob had passed every shooting and training course, carried a gun, and was a valuable member of the team. Sometimes local guys would be speaking to me in Arabic, while Rob was nearby, not letting on that he could understand what they were saying. Rob would often turn to me and say, "That guy is full of shit," and he usually turned out to be right. Rob was funny, he worked hard, and he was always willing to help out. He is still like that.

Our main goal at that time was to protect US Embassy workers and get the personnel who needed to travel outside the Green Zone to their meetings and back safely.

At that time, ministries and other government buildings were reopening. Any US personnel who were there to help the Iraqis get things up and running needed protection when they traveled outside the Green Zone in the city.

While these trips were routine, Rob remembers the tension of going into Red Zone areas: "You never knew what to expect," he said. "Even in the practice runs, the prep runs, the setup, it was so fluid, it was like you had to anticipate anything." Conditions were changing in Iraq: small-arms fire and rocket-propelled grenades had initially been the biggest threats, but now the enemy had gotten creative and was employing more car bombs and suicide bombs. "You could never relax," Rob said. "It was always a cat-and-mouse game." Rob was performing well and enjoying the work, but his thoughts were turning to home.

Rob's son, Adam, was born in July of 2009. Rob returned to Michigan the day after his son's birth and started a new tour in Iraq in September, promising his wife, Alia, that he would quit contracting work by December of 2010. "That was our plan," he said. "I still liked the work, but I needed to figure something else out because I also wanted to be there with my son, every day. I knew I was going to be missing stuff."

But things didn't go as planned. On October 25, 2009, Rob was wounded by a double suicide car bomb attack.

It happened at a ministry that Rob had been to many times before. "It was an ordinary venue that wasn't far from the Green Zone, by the second bridge on the Tigris River," he said. "It was still in Baghdad and not an especially hot area."

Rob's team was there doing advance work for a planned visit. Rob usually worked advance details, because his language skills were so helpful, and then was helping to provide exterior security.

"I was on Raven 14," Rob said. "We got there at about 9:30 a.m. and parked our vehicles where we normally parked at this ministry. It was right off the main road, surrounded by T walls [made of twelve-foot-high, portable, steel-reinforced concrete for blast protection], and had a metal gate that slides back and forth. The detail would eventually drive through the gate."

Rob went inside with a team leader for Raven 14 named Heath Chitwood, whom everyone called Val. "We went inside, and the designated marksmen went to set up on the roof while Val and I coordinated with their security guards and brought the canines in to sweep," Rob said. "Once everyone was in position, Val and I called in the clear on the inside of the building, and then we stood at the entrance of the building. I remember we were talking about both being ready for a break."

Security appeared to be tighter than normal, Rob said. "There were usually five or six local guys providing security by the front, but on this morning, it seemed as though double that number of guys were standing around."

Rob and Val talked about the unusual number of local guards, but they didn't think much of it. Rob wondered if maybe the ministry had just hired some new guys for security.

"Then we heard an explosion go off at the Ministry of Justice, which was near Bridge 4, about a quarter of a mile away," Rob said. "We could feel the vibration and then we heard small-arms fire. We radioed it in, but even that was not extra alarming."

As anyone who has spent time downrange in Iraq at that time will tell you, the thunder of a distant explosion was not out of the ordinary. Radio vehicles would let them know where it was coming from.

Rob said he just thought, "God, that was a loud one," when he heard the firefight that morning. But his detail was close to the Green Zone and his comfort level was high.

That didn't last. Thirty seconds later, Rob heard small-arms fire that sounded much closer, right outside the building. He was facing away from the ministry, looking toward the gate, and Val was facing the building, talking on the radio.

A second car bomb detonated, but this one was right in front of them. "It was almost like something you would see in a movie, the way everything slowed way down," Rob said. "One minute I was looking out, with my sunglasses over my eyes and my earpiece in my ear. Then the bomb went off. The first thing I saw was a huge flame rising over the gate. Then the shock waves came over and under the gate, rolling right toward me as the gate disappeared. It was like watching a wave of heat move through the air."

When I think about how close Rob was to that explosion, it feels like a miracle that he's still here to talk about it. I have seen shock waves, and it's a strange and powerful thing, as though you are seeing something that isn't meant to be visible, but I know I've never seen anything like what Rob saw that day.

The ministry had been hit by a VBIED. A car had pulled up right outside, and the driver claimed that he had just broken down. "I heard that a local Iraqi guy gave authorization for these trucks to come through, so maybe it was an internal job. I don't know," Rob said. "But it didn't seem like most of their guys got hurt, aside from a few concussions."

It proved to be the most lethal double suicide bombing in four years: more than two hundred people died and nine hundred were wounded, most of them locals. Rob was within fifty meters of the explosive impact, as close as I can imagine someone being and still survive.

"I put my hand up to my face, defensively," Rob remembers, "and began to turn my head and body toward the right, away from the wave. The next thing I knew, it was just complete silence." Rob remembers talking to himself as he regained consciousness. "It was all in my own voice, and all in my mind, although it felt like it was happening out loud." Rob remembers asking, "What's going on?" Rob's own voice answered, "I don't know." "Are you dead?" Rob asked. "I don't know," Rob answered. Rob wondered, "Is this what happens when you die? Do you talk to yourself?"

As Rob began to regain consciousness, he found himself in the middle of utter chaos, but he couldn't open his eyes. "There had been no sound other than my own voice," Rob said. "But, slowly, I started to get my hearing back. I could hear screaming and crying, but at first it seemed distant. Then I became aware of my hands and knees. I was facedown, but I realized that I had gone through something physical, maybe like a frame. Whatever it was was keeping me partially suspended. In other words, my chest and arms were hanging over something, almost as though I had gone through a window frame and stopped. I still don't know if that's what it was." Rob's first conscious thought was about his infant son, Adam, and Rob felt a strong need to see him.

"I put my hands up to my face and it felt slimy; I thought maybe I was burned," Rob said. He still couldn't see and he remembers thinking, "You've got to get up; you've got to move."

Rob was disoriented and thought he was in the same position he had been in before the explosion. "I turned to my left, trying to remember the path of the perimeter of the facility, thinking that I could follow it from memory," he said. "It felt like I was standing up on top of a hill, but the ground was loose and shifting under my feet." Rob's vision was still black, so he extended his hands in front of him as he walked tentatively forward; soon he felt something like a wall.

"I was trying to feel my way, and I wanted to keep going to my left," Rob said. "The path seemed clear, except sometimes I would hit something that felt like cables, so I would grab them or duck under whatever seemed to be hanging down. Eventually, I stopped and just stood there and tried to get my bearings. I could hear people walking around me and screaming, louder now. Everything I heard was in Arabic and I didn't know who anyone was."

Rob found his voice and started calling for Val, who had been standing within two feet of Rob at the moment of the explosion. There was no answer.

Rob knew that he needed to get out of there, but as more of

his senses began to return, he became less sure of what to do. "It was as though different possible threats kept emerging as I became more conscious of my surroundings. I wasn't feeling any pain yet, if you can believe it," he said.

As Rob tried to make sense of his situation, he heard his teammates on his radio. "I realized that my earpiece was still in my ear. It wasn't Val speaking. I wanted to respond, so I felt for where I normally clipped my mic, but that wasn't there any longer. I start feeling around on my body, trying to find my radio so that I could grab my mic wire and respond to the radio call. I said that I was still inside but that I didn't know my exact location, that I couldn't see, and that I couldn't find Val. But then I heard the voices through the earpiece again and they told me to hold on and not move; they were going to come and get me. They said they were still inside the building, and to hold on."

Then Rob heard a voice near him, a man speaking Arabic. "He was saying, 'Someone help this guy,'" Rob remembers, "but no one was responding to him. He sounded like a local. His voice got louder as he approached me, and, speaking in Arabic, he told me to give him my hand." Rob hesitated and then held out his hand. The stranger guided Rob down a hill until he was on level ground. Rob didn't know it, but he was climbing down a pile of bodies.

"Am I outside or inside?" asked Rob, who still couldn't see.

"You're outside," the man told him.

"Sit tight; we're coming," Rob heard the voice say through his earpiece, in English.

After they had walked a few steps on what felt like flat ground, the man stopped. "Walk straight ahead," he told Rob, "until you feel water." Rob wondered why there was water outside. He learned later that the explosion had dug a crater in the ground so deep that it caused the water lines to burst. But in that moment, it made no sense that water would be flowing in the desert. He could hear people running around and speaking in Arabic.

"We've got eyes on you; hang tight," said the voice in English on his earpiece. Right then, an American soldier came over and guided Rob back to the vehicles across the street. "Be careful as you step over the water," he told Rob. "There are electrical wires hanging down."

A medic began cleaning Rob's face. Rob still couldn't see anything.

"Doc, Val is dead," Rob told the man working on his face.

"No, he's not," the medic told him. "I think he's in the follow vehicle." Rob wasn't sure whether to believe him.

Rob and Val were blown apart from one another, so they didn't get a chance to compare notes until much later. That's when Rob found out that when Val regained consciousness after the explosion he could see but couldn't hear. "It was the reverse of the state I was in, and we both thought the other one was dead."

As Rob began to become aware of the gravity of his wounds, he asked the medic about them. "Tell me the truth," Rob demanded back at the main camp in Baghdad. "I don't care, just tell me how bad it is."

All Rob remembers is wanting to regain his sight and to see his son. The team needed an escort to take them to Balad Air Base, about forty miles north of Baghdad. Rob doesn't remember a whole lot about the transportation until the medevac helicopter that was carrying him approached the hospital where he was to be treated.

"I started hurting," he said. "I realized that my wrist was

killing me and that I had the most intense pressure on the top of my head."

It may sound strange, but Rob was incredibly lucky. When the hospital staff removed Rob's watch from his wrist at the hospital in Balad, they saw that shrapnel had pierced the center of the watch, suggesting that the watch may have protected him by deflecting a bullet.

Rob had asked his teammates to call his brother in Michigan while he was on the way to the hospital. Rob's uncle was working with a construction company at the US Embassy in Baghdad, and he traveled to Balad when he heard Rob had been hurt.

"My uncle was there when I regained consciousness in the hospital," Rob said. "He helped me call my mother and my wife."

The incident was all over the news, and Rob's wife had been trying to contact him all day, without success. "I didn't want anyone to call my wife yet, because I wanted to be the one to call her," he said.

When the two finally did connect, Rob told her he had been a little beat up.

The truth was that his wounds were extensive. He had suffered a U-shaped gash on his head that was filled with debris, his eyelids were lacerated and hung over his eyes, his nose was deeply cut, three of his lumbar discs had ruptured, and his hearing and vision were both impaired.

"I had stitches and scars all over my face and my face was blown up like a balloon, but I still had all my limbs and I could walk," Rob said.

Soon after, he returned home to the United States and

began to work with neurologists, ophthalmologists, physical therapists, and speech therapists to try to get back into fighting shape.

"My goal was to get back and go downrange for one more mission," he said. "I wanted to leave contracting on my own two feet."

Rob initially felt optimistic about this, even though he was crawling up stairs at home because it was too painful to walk up them. And his waking hours centered on trying to regain his health, which proved to be no easy task.

"I had to see so many doctors, it was like a full-time job, and I had to fight to see particular doctors and specialists. I ultimately had to work with a lawyer to get the insurance company to acknowledge my disability and facilitate my medical care." The stress was taking a toll on Rob: he said he felt "frustrated and angry, all the time." Rob's doctors told him it was unlikely he would be able to return to security work.

But that December, Rob got job offers from the Secret Service and the Federal Air Marshal Service. "The job offers came in December, and they wanted me to start in January in DC," Rob said, sighing. "All that testing, all my plans were finally paying off, and I had to call and tell them what had happened. Of course, the agencies would require a new clearance, which I wasn't sure I would get, and they couldn't guarantee that there would be a job waiting for me if and when I got a new clearance."

Rob felt useless. "I had been in the best shape of my life, constantly going a hundred miles an hour, and all of a sudden I was in pain and physically limited. That hit me really hard."

All Rob remembers wanting to do was to get back to normal, and he resisted the idea that he and his family might need to define a new normal. "I had been the breadwinner, and now my wife had to go back to work," he said. "Our son was a few months old. I went into a serious depression. I was really angry at the world and not the easiest person to get along with. My wife and I had a rough two-year patch, because on top of the physical changes I was dealing with, I felt useless not working. The whole situation made me so angry and depressed. I am blessed she stuck by me."

Rob found it difficult to accept help. "My mom used to come over to try to help with the baby, and I would say, 'I got this' and send her home, because I wanted to be useful," he said. "I felt like I had a duty to contribute something, and I couldn't stand the idea of people feeling sorry for me."

Rob's faith ultimately helped him chart a new course. He still doesn't know how to interpret his out-of-body experience in the immediate aftermath of the blast. He still doesn't know whether he was dead. "It was so quiet, just me and my voice, like nothing I had ever seen or experienced before," he said. "I don't know if it was a moment with God or why it was all in my voice."

Rob accepts that his experience may remain a mystery but believes that everything happens for a reason. "I think God did not want me to finish that contract," he said. "Maybe something else would have happened, something worse. God was telling me, 'It's time to go home and be with your family.'"

Thinking about his son, who was six weeks old at the time of the blast, "is what pulled me through," Rob said. "I had to get up so that I could go see him."

It took two years for Rob to accept that he needed to set a new goal. Back in Michigan, he and his wife established a car company, which is thriving.

Rob has undergone three back surgeries and he still struggles with his vision, but he is able to drive and read and see his loved ones.

The bombing damaged nerves and compromised feeling in his right foot, but he can walk and, with some adjustments, run. Rob fired a pistol for the first time since the accident recently, but it was much harder than it had been before the blast because his right eye is no longer dominant, which changes his ability to aim. Other things have changed, too. "I am a little bit more patient than I used to be, and I'm learning how to have a normal life again," he said.

"I loved the action of working overseas, I loved the adrenaline, and I loved the brotherhood. It is a tough job to transition out of, especially when I felt like it took me a while to find it in the first place, but I always want to be independent and self-sufficient, and that keeps me motivated to keep moving down a new path."

Rob said he feels blessed to be running a successful business, but sometimes he has feelings of doubt: "I think, 'Is this right? Is this enough?' I want to keep going because I'm not satisfied."

Rob is working to keep his business growing and training to run a marathon. "I'm accepting where I am, and keeping my sights on where I need to be," he said. "It might take me longer to get there, but I know I'll do it."

The mass-carnage event that Rob survived was something that most people have experienced only in the movies. It is amazing that he is still alive, and that his spirit is intact. It would be easy for someone in Rob's position to become bitter and withdrawn, but Rob is neither.

He even said that he would deploy again, if he could, and if, he joked, "my wife wouldn't divorce me."

It didn't surprise me to learn that Rob started a company that has become successful. I've watched him learn one new profession from scratch and saw how dedicated he was to making sure he got it right. His commitment to being a good husband, father, and person is also apparent to anyone who knows him. That might be his most impressive quality.

Rob is just one member of a whole category of people who have put their lives on the line and sacrificed for the United States without getting the recognition or benefits that are routinely accorded to veterans.

Rob's face and head bear some scars, but his struggle is not otherwise visible, and he prefers to keep it that way. "Most people won't ask about the scars, so they don't know what happened unless I reveal it, and I am pretty closed off about it," he said. "I don't need recognition."

Rob isn't the kind of guy who wants to be in the spotlight. "I served my country and I love my country, but I don't think the United States owes me anything," he said.

"I loved what I was doing, I loved my brothers, and I think we were taking risks for something that matters. I have been blessed."

GOOD CHARACTER

Rob more than fulfilled his duty as a contractor, but, to me, his story also illustrates the power of upholding obligations in your private life. Duty exists not only in the workplace. Rob struggled hard to figure out how to reorganize his life because he felt a deep sense of obligation to be a responsible husband and father, and a self-sufficient, contributing member of society.

I have obligations to my family, my friends, and my community. I have a duty to be honorable and trustworthy, to contribute, and to not let my loved ones down in their moments of need. Sharing a household with other people comes with obligations to help keep that house running smoothly: to make sure the bills are paid, the property is maintained, and the people living under that roof have what they need. It might sound a little strange to think of a household as a team, but I think being in a strong marriage or having a well-functioning family requires teamwork.

We all have a duty to work and to contribute to society, to not be a burden on society. That does not mean that you might not encounter hard times or have moments when you might need some assistance. Your duty, if you are getting help, is to figure out a way to get off the assistance, and maybe even get yourself into a position to pay it back by helping others.

I believe we also have a duty to make sure the teams we belong to are honorable. I wish that more people would stand up and report bullshit when they see it. One of the reasons that I have continued to speak about the events in Benghazi on September 11, 2012, is that I believe we all have a duty to tell the truth. We have an obligation to report deficiencies and immoral behavior in our workplaces and to try to correct them in our communities.

My brothers and I stood up to tell the truth about Benghazi because politicians were trying to cover up the circumstances of the deaths that night. We could not let that stand. If something is not right and no one speaks up, nothing will get fixed, and things may get worse. It sucks to sacrifice a career for the truth. It was not easy to hear people call us liars when we knew we were not. But it would have been much worse had someone else died or been injured because we didn't speak up.

EMBRACING THE VALUES
DUTY

Duty might seem like a grim value, not something exciting or classically heroic like courage or integrity. But duty is an essential value, in the same way that the ability to exercise willpower is an essential skill. Let's face it: sometimes you have to do what has to be done, even if it's going to be hard, and even if there is something else you would rather be doing. In Ranger School, we used to call that "embracing the suck," and the practice of fulfilling your obligations—or doing your duty—has benefits beyond what you actually get done.

Sometimes it seems like it's getting harder for some people to set aside their own egos. For most of us, we are part of a team, both at work and at home. And you should try to think of yourself as part of a larger team, too, as part of a larger community or series of communities. You have duties to each one of those teams. Teamwork is not about drinking together or going to parties together. You can build camaraderie by socializing, but that is not teamwork. Teamwork is fulfilling your obligations and, in so doing, upholding the values of the organization.

Most of us neither live nor work in isolation, and when someone in our chain of relationships fails to do their duty, we all feel it sooner or later. When you fulfill your duties, it is helpful to think of yourself as contributing to a larger mission that might have more meaning for you. For example, instead of thinking, "I'm taking the trash out," you can reframe that duty to think, "I am taking care of my home and my family." And that is the truth. If everyone just stops executing all the annoying little chores and duties that come with keeping a home, see how long it takes before that home becomes unpleasant and then unlivable.

Doing your duty usually means that you are contributing to a team. You never know what the outcome will be and what your team can accomplish together. Heroes never ask to be heroes. You put yourself in a position and you do your job and sometimes that's the way it works out.

The teamwork is essential. No one puts themselves above that team, or that mission. I believe that our team was successful in Benghazi because no one put themselves above anyone else.

Exercise Your Willpower

The way the duties are apportioned in any particular team is personal. I know that a person who stays home with their kids is doing hard work. There were times when I came home between deployments and stayed home with my kids while my wife was working, and those were challenging days. My point here is not that one type of household arrangement is necessarily better than another, only that duties do not have to be exactly the same among team members.

The process of employing your willpower to fulfill your obligations—I mean using your sheer grit, over and over—will teach you to expect more of yourself. Willpower is like a muscle. There is a lot of research confirming that your willpower gets stronger every time you use it, but you don't need to read, study, or over-think it. Just start trying. If you mess up, don't use that failure as an excuse to give up. Reset your sights and try again. Knowing you have the self-control to do what needs to be done gives you confidence. But you have to build it up. Have faith and get started.

CHAPTER FIVE

RESPECT

Treat people as they should be treated. In the Soldier's Code, we pledge to "treat others with dignity and respect while expecting others to do the same." Respect is what allows us to appreciate the best in other people. Respect is trusting that all people have done their jobs and fulfilled their duty. And self-respect is a vital ingredient with the Army value of respect, which results from knowing you have put forth your best effort. The Army is one team and each of us has something to contribute.

I AM WILLING TO RISK MY LIFE for other people even though I may not respect one or more of them. Why am I willing to give my life for someone I don't respect? Because I respect life itself; I respect our common humanity and our right to live our lives in freedom; I respect another person's individual right to live unless and until I think they have the intent and opportunity to kill me or someone else.

While I do think that everyone is entitled to basic respect and dignity by virtue of being human, I also believe that we earn additional respect through our actions. I respect the men and women who have stood by me in situations where we were being attacked. I respect my fellow Rangers for their toughness, their integrity, and their willingness to sacrifice themselves. I know what they went through to earn the Ranger tab and Scroll.

On an individual level, some of my brothers put themselves at a disadvantage to help me succeed. Someone took part of my load when I was falling out on a march and allowed me to finish. Guys waited for me after an airborne jump when I landed in a drop zone and was struggling to find my way to the rally point. The guys who helped me were already carrying heavy loads and they could have gone faster, but they waited for me and guided me. They sacrificed themselves to help me, and I respect their conduct.

Treating all people with a basic level of respect is not only ethical; it is also civil and pragmatic. And I mean treating all people with respect, not just the people whom you know and like.

"I Met an American, and He Wasn't So Bad"

When I was deploying in Afghanistan and Iraq, there were some guys I worked with who displayed an attitude of reflexive mistrust toward the locals. I understood their suspicion, but I did not think it was productive. In my experience, when I was respectful to the locals, they were generally respectful to me. There was tension on both sides, and it was not always warranted.

When I was making routine stops in Kabul, for example, shopping in a bazaar or stopping in a coffee shop, the proprietor or the other customers might bristle a bit when I walked in or they might look me up and down in a guarded way. I found that it defused the tension if I smiled and tried to speak a bit of their language, even just to say hello or please or thank you.

If I offered a handshake or put a hand over my heart when I was leaving, which is a local custom, I usually got a smile or some respectful acknowledgment in return. I like to think that treating the locals with respect made somebody think, "Hey, I met an American, and he wasn't so bad."

If treating people with respect can help defuse tension, it follows that treating others with a lack of respect can increase tension. When I was working in Tripoli in 2012, five of us drove out of town on a rare day off to see the ruins of Leptis Magna, which had been an important city in Libya during the Carthaginian Empire.

Our group included two guys from the contractor, Global Resource Solutions (GRS), and three US government employees, officials with papers from the State Department. We traveled separately as we returned to Tripoli at the end of the day. I rode with the contractors and one of the US officials, and the two other officials traveled in another car. Just as our car arrived at the Annex in Tripoli, the two US officials in the other car called us on the radio and said, "We are stuck at a checkpoint; we need QRF assistance." QRF stands for quick reaction force, and that is what people radio for if they are in trouble.

We got on the phone and asked them if guns were drawn. The two officials said, "No, not yet, but they're getting antsy because we won't let them in the car or roll down the windows to talk to them."

I said, "You need to communicate with them," but the officials refused, arguing, "We can't communicate with them if they might get hostile."

Our team understood what was happening, and since there were no guns drawn, we told QRF they could stand down and that we would go and check the situation out informally.

We drove toward the spot where they had been stopped. It was a snap checkpoint, which can pop up out of nowhere. The militia members who had established the checkpoint controlled that road.

I remember thinking, "What do the US officials expect the checkpoint guards to do?" That was their road. They could shut it down any time they wanted. We had no control over that. If we decided to drive on it, we had to at least make an effort to talk to them, to show that we respected their position.

I am not naïve. That militia could have been doing a little intel, getting the make of our vehicles and checking us out. If that was the case, guess what? If you are already there, it's done. Show the locals some respect and get out. Some of the locals spoke a bit of English, so these guys could have tried displaying their State Department papers and saying something like, "We apologize, we didn't know this was closed off."

It was not abnormal for working foreigners to be going about their business in Libya, trying to get home at the end of the day. The odds are excellent that this militia would have waved them through.

I called our guys again and asked if they had managed to communicate the fact that they were with the State Department. They said no, and I could tell from their voices that they were starting to panic. As we drove up, I could see that five militia members had surrounded their car; they were pulling on the car doors and speaking loudly, but they didn't have their guns out and the situation didn't seem out of control. The guards wanted to talk to the guys in the car.

We pulled up behind them, but we didn't roll up hard or come charging up like we were the cavalry. I had a pistol, but I didn't want the militia to get their guns out and shoot. I displayed my embassy badge, identified myself, and asked what was going on. We verified that the guys in the car were with us. The militia members consulted with one another and said they understood, and they let the car pass.

Everything was defused and no one had raised a weapon. Could that situation have gone the other way? Yes. Could the militia have turned out to be hostile? Sure. We were taking a calculated risk. Displaying basic respect for the locals controlling the roads, in the same way we expected it on roads that we controlled, seemed like a reasonable move. The case officers had displayed disrespect by refusing to communicate with the locals, and the consequences could have been severe.

Showing respect doesn't mean rolling over. It is important to know when it is appropriate to take a hard line. There was a fender bender between a vehicle being driven by US Army military intelligence (MI) personnel and a vehicle driven by Afghani locals in Kabul in 2007 that escalated quickly. The MI personnel, in a panic, called for any QRF nearby for backup. There must have been about thirty of us on the back roads, and as we raced toward the scene, I remember seeing the local militia confidently banging on this US car, yelling, waving weapons, and trying to break in and get our MI guys out of their car. We had ten civilian-style cars screeching to a stop and surrounding this volatile scene from every direction. We got out hard with all our kits and rifles, demanding that they let our people go. The faces of those militiamen were priceless. They knew they had to let our guys move forward.

SELF-RESPECT

Self-respect is a precondition for earning the respect of other people. No one is perfect, certainly not I. I have made many poor choices and done things that lacked integrity, many of which I recounted in my book *The Ranger Way* (Hachette

Book Group, 2017). I have tried to take responsibility for my actions and learn from my mistakes, which are key components of self-respect. You are worthy of respect even if you are not perfect. I have fallen down and picked myself back up many times, and I am a stronger person, a better father, and a better partner for my failures.

We were able to keep our people safe in Tripoli and Kabul because we were confident in our ability to assess each situation and respond appropriately. The same principle applies to an individual trying to overcome a failure or cultivate self-respect.

Honesty is an important dimension of self-respect, in the sense that you need to figure out who you are and how to be yourself in order to have true self-respect. I don't care if you don't like the way I dress, or if you disagree with my politics, or even if you think I am a prima donna. I know who I am. I know my strengths and my weaknesses; working to improve both of them is a form of self-respect.

Everyone is not good at everything. But everyone has something to contribute. When I am leading a team, my priority is to identify people's strengths and help them to develop their skills and make their best contribution to the team. In the Army, or in a contracting assignment, that might mean asking: Is one team member stronger or faster than everyone else? Is somebody especially good at IT? Is someone a gifted mechanic? People have strengths, and good leaders figure out how to use them. A team is strongest when each member is contributing to the mission from their most powerful position. That experience benefits the individual team members. When people are recognized for things that they are genuinely good at, they develop self-confidence and the motivation to strengthen their skills. That creates self-respect.

Identifying strengths also creates opportunities to exchange information. Among Rangers, we cross-train each other in our strong skills. The time and effort we spend teaching each other brings the team together and increases our proficiency as a group.

In the special forces community, each team has its own function, and everyone is specialized within the team, but we do learn from each other and can be prepared to jump in for one another if it is needed. When people are self-confident, they won't be intimidated if someone else is better at a particular skill. Rangers and other members of the special ops communities tend to inspire one another as much as intimidate, and that is what allows us to succeed.

BEN MORGAN

Ben Morgan went to high school in Fruita, Colorado, which is a part of Grand Valley, near Grand Junction, where I'm from. Ben is only a couple of years younger than I am, but we didn't know each other well in high school. If you had asked me then, I would have predicted that Ben would stay a hometown boy and be the life of every hard party in Grand Junction. I certainly never would have guessed that we would both wind up being Army Rangers. It turns out there was a lot that I didn't know about Ben.

Ben lives in Colorado today, but he is actually from just about everywhere. He was born in Texas and has moved about forty times. His dad was a helicopter pilot in Vietnam and then flew professionally for forty years in the oil industry in Texas and Louisiana when Ben was small and later as far away as Saudi Arabia. The Morgan family moved five times before Ben started kindergarten, and Ben did not arrive in Colorado until he was in eighth grade.

"I didn't know anybody in eighth grade," Ben recalls. "I had one friend and he had lunch at a different time, so I would go to the main office at school and tell them I had a detention so I wouldn't have to sit alone in the cafeteria. I remember feeling bored and overwhelmed by school."

Ben started drinking in high school: "Once I started drinking, I felt as though people liked me and I liked myself more." Soon Ben's drinking habit had spiraled well beyond what I might have called typical among students our age. Ben was drinking almost every day on the way to school, at school, and after school. "Weekends were for extreme excess," he told me, "like a fifth of vodka by myself and then eight or ten beers on Friday and Saturday night. My parents were worried about me, but I don't think they had any idea how much and how often I was drinking."

Second and Third Chances

As Ben got older, his drinking and careless behavior resulted in a couple of very dangerous car accidents. "I got into a half dozen minor fender benders, sometimes when other people were driving," he recalled, "but eventually I had a really bad car accident. My girlfriend was asleep in the passenger seat of my 1970s Toyota Land Cruiser, which had no safety features, and I passed out and drove off the road while I was driving to another party, and I hit a brick mailbox, telephone pole, fence, and utility box. It felt miraculous that we were okay, and later that night I told my mom that maybe I had a problem with alcohol."

It was the first time that Ben had spoken those words or started to think about what they might mean. But Ben was still a teenager, and he thought that he would just change his ways on his own. "I woke up the next day all wound up from the adrenaline of the accident, but then we never really got to the bottom of my behavior," he said, "and my concern kind of wore off."

When Ben was seventeen, he and his buddies got drunk, broke into a car, and led the local police on a wild chase when they were spotted. The assistant district attorney and the sheriff were willing to take a risk, and put Ben in a "scared straight" diversion program, which required him to spend two eight-hour days in the state penitentiary in Cañon City.

"I had to go for an eight-hour visit each time, and I spent those eight hours shadowing an actual inmate," he said. "I had to tell him my story and then he told me his story, and then I spent the day with him, seeing the reality of where I was heading. My inmate counselor's sentence was for decades. When he told me about his experience, which involved a drug deal that went bad and ended violently, I could totally see it happening to me. I ate my meals with the inmates and had to go with them as they moved throughout the prison, to their cells, the bathrooms, everywhere.

"There were no guards escorting me. There were guards in the prison, but I didn't know how long it would take them to get to me if something happened, and they made sure I knew that. It was scary as hell. Everyone felt dangerous. My inmate counselor would tell me, very matter-of-factly, this one is a rapist, that one's in for murder, this guy is insane. I remember there was one enormous guy in the yard, and my counselor said, 'Wait, let me walk in front of you when we pass him; he's not right.' I was terrified."

The worst day was the one where he had to return to the prison and spend the day shadowing an inmate with one of his parents. "My dad went with me, and he is a tough guy," Ben said. "He served in the Vietnam War. But he told me afterward that he had never been more afraid in his life than he was that day. I felt bad about that. The worst part is that I figured he must have been thinking, 'How did my son become such a fucking loser?'"

Ben was chastened by the prison visits, but they were still not enough for him to permanently change his ways. He started drinking again, slowly increasing his intake back to his old, excessive ways. Ben graduated from high school in 1992, just barely. "I was probably something like second-to-last in a class of more than two hundred students" he said. "I'm guessing the school said, 'Hell, let's let him graduate and be rid of him.'"

After graduating, Ben stayed local, doing odd jobs to support what was still a serious drinking habit, and enrolling at Colorado Northwestern Community College in Rangely, but his study habits were weak and he only lasted one semester.

"I just drank and played video games and acted like an idiot," he said.

Following the Family Tradition

Ben decided to join the military, as many of his relatives had done. Both of Ben's parents had served in Vietnam, Ben's mom as a nurse and his dad as a helicopter pilot for a medevac unit.

Ben had one uncle in the Ranger Regiment, another uncle had been in Vietnam, and another uncle had been a helicopter pilot in the Marine Corps (he flew people out of Vietnam during the fall of Saigon). One of Ben's grandfathers had served in the Navy during World War II, and his other grandfather served in World War II, Korea, and Vietnam. Ben's great-great-grandfather served in the Army during World War I, and Ben has relatives who served in the Civil War and the American Revolution.

"You'd think I would have had a very sober, realistic view of military life," he said, "and in some ways I did, but I was also dumb as all get-out. I knew there were bad people in the world, and part of me thought it would be exciting to just go kill bad guys."

Ben did well on the entrance test for the Army and joined up to try to be an FO. That's a forward observer, the spotter who directs air strikes on to a target. He also thought he might want to be a Ranger, like his uncle. "I think my parents probably threw a party when I left for basic training," he told me. "I feel bad for everything I put my parents through. There was no reason for it. I know there is often some trauma behind bad behavior when you peel it back, but there wasn't any of that in my home. I can't blame my parents."

Ben got a little surprise when he got to his meet-up point in Denver to enlist. "The Army put us up in a hotel that was very familiar to me," he said. "It was the site of one of the wildest parties my friends and I had ever been to. Looking back now, it seems inconceivable that a hotel would let teenagers shut down an entire floor...for two days and let us party like wild animals. It was one of the craziest things I'd ever seen, let alone experienced."

"You Lied...Go Home"

It was a bad omen. When Ben had filled out the paperwork to enlist, he had been asked if he had ever been in any kind of legal trouble. Ben's juvenile record was supposed to have been expunged, so he didn't think he had to disclose that information, and he didn't. Somehow, Ben's history came up anyway, which made him guilty of fraudulent enlistment.

"They called me in to the MEPS [Military Entrance Processing Station] in downtown Denver and basically said, 'You lied, pack your shit and go home,'" Ben said. "They said I could resubmit an application for a waiver to rejoin the Army in six months, if I didn't have any additional trouble. I had to call my dad and tell him that they were putting me on a bus and I was coming back home. I felt like such an idiot. I couldn't even join the Army."

Ben had been on the cusp of turning over a new leaf, but now he felt jinxed, as though he had screwed up so badly in the past that his future could not be fixed. He returned home and started to drink again.

Ben wasn't breaking into people's cars or houses anymore, but he got a crappy job delivering pizzas and spent his downtime drinking and partying with friends.

"It was a bad life," he said flatly, "and I knew that I had to change something, but I just felt stuck, like I was in this limbo. The Army seemed like my only hope, and even that didn't seem like a sure thing."

Ben was living with friends across the street from a local college, and described his home as a nonstop party.

"It was probably the worst environment I could have put myself in," he said. "The house was so nasty that my mother would not set foot in it. One particularly rowdy night, the police showed up and ended up writing us a ticket for having a disorderly house. I had to go to court and pay a fine for that. I remember thinking that I was screwed and now I would not be able to get back into the Army."

Luckily for Ben, he only received a fine and the Army did not seem to care.

Finally, at age twenty, Ben was able to reenlist. This time Ben went in as an 11 Bravo, an infantry guy. Instead of concentrating on drinking, he refocused his energy on basic training. "I went twelve weeks without a drink, and I didn't even care," he said. "I wanted to be good at my job, and I started to develop more self-respect as I figured out what I was good at."

Ben didn't stop drinking altogether after basic training. "I would still have a drink on the weekends or a day off, but it was different," he said. "I wasn't blacking out. I wasn't drinking in the morning, or during the day. I replaced my drinking behavior in the Army with exercise and training and chores and all the other things they were making us do. And I realized that I didn't need to drink."

A Changed Life

Ben went through basic training, advanced individual training, Jump School, and the Ranger Indoctrination Program (RIP), and he absorbed the values of the Ranger Creed. "Becoming an Army Ranger is what really changed my life," Ben told me. "I wanted to help and be part of the team. I wanted to be as good as I could be."

Part of being as good as he could be was accepting that everybody has to do their job in the Army or else nothing works. "I didn't ever want to be the reason anyone failed or had to do extra work," Ben said. "Earning the respect of the other members of my platoon was important to me."

One of the many things that I admire about Ben is how totally self-effacing he is about what he accomplished. "Putting the hours in and keeping up the can-do attitude, you know what spits out at the end of the day?" he asked me. "An average Ranger."

But Ben wanted to be a better-than-average Ranger. "I was probably an average guy in Ranger Battalion, and it took a lot of effort to be average, but I always wanted to be better. And no matter how hard I pushed myself, someone else was always better. The funny thing was, it wasn't discouraging in that environment. That was part of what I loved about it. If I ran a 5:15 mile and someone else ran it in five minutes, then a five-minute mile became the new goal. If someone else did it, it just seemed possible."

I understand exactly what Ben means. There were a few genetic freaks of nature in the regiment, but most Rangers are regular soldiers working their asses off. It sounds basic, but it is very powerful to be in a group of people who share this mind-set. Ben saw that he could get better if he worked harder.

It wasn't all smooth sailing. Ben got the same rough treatment and mind-fucking that everyone who goes through RIP gets. "Maybe I can't do this," he remembered thinking at the beginning, when the intimidation factor tends to be especially high. "I wasn't going to quit, though," he said. "It was more like all the smoking we got made me mad, because I didn't want to give anyone the satisfaction of having made me quit."

"If He Can Do It, I Can Too"

Ben also looked at the guys who were succeeding and thought, "I know this dude, and he's not Superman. If he can do it, I can too."

A week after Ben finished the Indoctrination Program in 1994, his unit was ordered to deploy to Haiti. The Battle of Mogadishu, in Somalia, during which two Black Hawk helicopters were shot down, had taken place a few months earlier, in October 1993. The graphic consequences of the Battle of Mogadishu, after which the bodies of American soldiers were dragged through the streets by local militia and civilians, were fresh in everyone's mind. Ben's uncle was the senior fire support officer for the regiment, and he happened to be on the ship with Ben in the hours before they left to start the mission.

"My uncle came over that night to talk to me for a few minutes. I was kind of scared," Ben said. "I was scared of possibly getting hurt or killed, but I actually think I was more terrified of making a mistake. I really didn't want to screw up. We talked, and I focused on what I knew to be true: Rangers are the best in the world at what we do. No matter what happens to me, if I am injured or killed, I will not be left. We will come back for one another."

At the last minute, the mission was called off. Ben was surprised to discover that he felt disappointed. Ben turned out to be a peacetime Ranger. He worked as a Ranger in the United States primarily as a trainer until 1997 and then again from 2003 to 2006. Between 1998 and 2003, Ben finished college at Colorado State University, worked as a member of ROTC, and met Leann, a doctoral student at the University of Northern Colorado, who would eventually become his wife.

Trying to Find a Balance

In 2007, Ben was working in Iraq as a contractor, as an instructor in a facility where Americans and Iraqi forces would train together. He and Leann had become parents to infant twins, a boy and a girl, in 2006. He and his wife had agreed that he would return home that fall. Ben, trying to balance work with responsibilities at home, would take brief assignments on State Department contracts to train battalion-level staff officers of host countries.

These assignments were usually in Malawi and Nigeria for two to three weeks at a time. "It didn't feel dangerous, per se," he said. "We really stood out, and locals would stare at us, but it was more a feeling of curiosity or suspicion, not hostility." Ben wanted to work for a federal agency, as many of his friends and former Rangers were doing. He went through physical tests, psychological interviews, and security clearance processes for multiple agencies and departments, but his history of risk-taking behavior was a problem.

"I Was a Wild, Reckless Kid"

"I was totally honest about my history, because I knew all of that behavior was truly in my past," he said. "I was a wild, reckless kid. It wasn't who I was anymore. I was taking responsibility for my past, and I was proud of how much I had changed and confident that I could do this work."

The federal agencies did not agree, which frustrated Ben. "I felt 100 percent changed," he told me. "I knew guys doing those jobs. There was no doubt in my mind that I could do that work and never have a problem. It was a kick in the gut."

In 2008, Ben's wife, Leann, got offered a teaching job at the

University of Texas at Tyler, so they moved to Texas and Ben decided to keep contracting.

By this time, the Army was so busy that it had begun outsourcing certain kinds of training in the United States. Ben took a job in Arkansas training soldiers who were preparing to deploy to Iraq. "It was a good program and a great group of guys running it," he said. "I was probably the least experienced instructor there."

Meanwhile, Ben had started to develop a painful sensation in his feet and, in true Ranger fashion, ignored it while he was working in Arkansas. "I thought I would see a specialist when I got some time off, and I kept putting it off," he said. Even as the pain worsened, he continued to put the job first.

Soon the job changed. While working in Arkansas, Ben had been continuing to pursue ways of deploying overseas again.

He succeeded, landing a job with Triple Canopy, Inc., a private security company that had gotten a contract to provide high-threat protection for the State Department in Iraq.

Years earlier, Ben had been offered a contract job with the CIA, but he had been unable to accept it due to a prior obligation. He wanted to be considered for that contract again, but knew that some of the requirements had changed, and he thought that the Triple Canopy job would help him secure work for the CIA.

Ben liked the people he worked with on the high-threat protection contract and felt that the work was meaningful. "I felt like the job made a difference," Ben said. "I used to think that the only way this war is going to end is through diplomacy, and if I can help keep the diplomats safe, they can do their jobs and we can all get out of here sooner rather than later, and maybe that will keep a few guys from getting killed."

But the pain in Ben's feet was increasing, to the point that simply standing still felt like an endurance test. He searched for a solution every time he returned home to the United States on his thirty-day leaves. He tried different shoes, custom orthotics, massages, acupuncture, cortisone injections, and more. But nothing worked.

Finally, the pain became so bad that Ben had to leave work so that he could spend more time off his feet.

Ben didn't tell anyone at work why he was taking time off because he still hoped to resolve the issue and ultimately qualify for the CIA contract.

To make matters worse, Ben had sustained what he thought was a minor back injury in Iraq during a rocket attack, and he figured he could address it if he worked out a little harder in the gym. But he started to suffer back spasms that lasted hours and immobilized him.

A Grim Period

Finally, Ben decided he needed to see a doctor on his next trip home. An MRI showed that Ben had two bulging discs in his thoracic spine, which runs from the base of the neck to the abdomen. "I was getting shots and physical therapy, but my back wasn't fixed," he said. "I didn't want to go in-country and have people count on me and have a spasm at the wrong time."

This marked the beginning of a grim period for Ben, who had been incorrectly diagnosed with plantar fasciitis in both of his feet. "You take for granted that you need to power through pain, and I did, but this had been going on for years," he said. "I remember being in Iraq and having to stand watch on a doorway or stand out in the street, guarding a venue for a long period of time. That was the worst. I was wearing custom insoles, but I still felt like my feet were going to explode. That pain had never gone away."

Doctors prescribed pain medications and muscle relaxers, but Ben didn't like them. "The medications I tried just made me feel foggy, and they didn't really take the pain away. It was not a good sensation," he said.

"I'm probably lucky they didn't work well for me, given my history. I remember thinking about chewing them up, because I started to think maybe it would be better to just be high than to be in so much pain every day. I'm pretty sure I would have gone down that road if I hadn't had my wife and kids."

Throughout all this, Ben continued to pursue the clearance process for the CIA contract. He thought, "If I can just get my back better, I'll be able to take the pain in my feet. I could power through that like I had been, if that were the only thing."

Ben was doing his best, but his best had gotten pretty bad. "It was so frustrating," he said. "My back and feet were killing me and I was trying all these treatments, but I was still in constant pain. The pain and my lack of mobility interfered with everything, and I started to get depressed."

Ben's physical pain compounded the ordinary stress of having a young family. Ben felt like he was in a bad mood all the time. "My son and daughter were little then and they would want to do things with me, and I wanted to do things with them, but I was always in pain, so I was kind of a grumpy person to be around," he said.

"At the time, I thought I was being a man and handling everything, but in retrospect I know I was short with everyone and that it was hard on my family."

"I Certainly Could Not Be That Guy"

Finally, the company that had the contract with the CIA called and told Ben he was cleared to attend their selection course. It was the job Ben had been after for five years, but he knew he could not accept it. "As badly as I wanted to go, I knew that I was not physically able to do the job," he said. "If I had an issue with my back in the wrong situation, it could cost somebody their life. I couldn't be that irresponsible. I would not want to work with somebody that I could not trust 100 percent, and I certainly could not be that guy."

It's a fact of life that soldiers are often injured or recovering from something, and we usually tease each other about it, but I know it is difficult to be your best self when you're in pain.

Ben sees that clearly today. "It's hard to be creative, to pay attention to other people, or to contribute to the world around you" when you're in pain, he said. "It got to the point where I didn't want to go anywhere or do anything because my brain was so focused on how much pain I was in. It really puts you in a dark place when this goes on for years."

Ben was in his late thirties, but he felt so stressed physically that he thought he might as well be eighty years old.

He was also embarrassed by the fact that the source of his pain was hidden. "At my worst, I was essentially disabled," he said. "But I didn't have a visible wound. And I was so depressed, I almost felt like it would have been better if I had actually sustained a real wound in battle, something I could actually look at and see as the source of my pain."

In 2012, when he and his family moved back to Colorado, Ben began seeing new doctors, but the process of recovery remained slow. He began to seek alternative care: he tried chiropractic care, acupuncture, massage therapy, float therapy, dry needling, CBD oil, and yoga. "You name it, I tried it," he said. "The best results were from the float therapy and exercises that improved and maintained my core strength." It was not until 2016 that Ben finally started to get some relief from his back pain. And it was not until 2018, after undergoing a failed surgery for his feet, that he found a doctor who figured out that the nerves in Ben's feet had been damaged, and that the orthotics he had been using only magnified the pain.

The progress with his back pain and the new treatment for his feet changed Ben's life. "There was such an enormous change in my physical ability to do anything," he said. "After ten years of not being able to stand without pain in my feet and six years of back pain and spasms, all of a sudden I could stand in one place and talk to someone for thirty minutes or an hour without feeling excruciating pain; I could get out of bed and stand up straight. I could put my socks on without having to lie on the floor. It changed my whole outlook on life."

For the first time in a decade, Ben felt happy.

"Trying to Be a Better Version of Myself"

"I have failed way more often than I have succeeded," Ben told me cheerfully, "and I used to look at all the times in my life when I came up short and feel bad about them. But today I look at the disappointments as events that happened to me and I know that, without them, I wouldn't be where I am today."

Ben wrote down everything that was important to him and made a list of things he wanted to work on. "I'm learning to judge myself based on how I am doing today compared with where I used to be instead of measuring myself against anyone I know or some stranger on Instagram.

"I'm just trying to be a better version of myself. For example, I realize that I wasn't always patient with my children when they were little and I was in so much pain. I'm always going to be working at being a better parent, and I feel like working toward that also makes me a better person. I look at that list often, and every day I do something to improve an item on that list."

Ben is still guided by the principles of the Ranger Creed. "If you apply the Ranger Creed to the rest of your life, you'll be all right," he said. "If you do that, you will give 100 percent and then some to everything you do."

For Ben, that means doing more than what is expected of him at all times, and it doesn't have to be a massive change. "If you are told to clean the toilet, go ahead and clean the floor around the toilet as well," he said. "You can apply that principle to the way you take care of yourself, and it doesn't have to be massive: when you go to the gym, if you push yourself to do one more set or one more rep than you said you were going to, you'll be better for it."

Ben thinks a lot about the last lines of the Ranger Creed: "Readily will I display the intestinal fortitude required to fight on to the Ranger objective and complete the mission though I be the lone survivor."

"You Don't Give Up"

That means that the mission comes first. Ben adapts it to mean that his mission in life today is to be a better version of himself every day, just as it was when he was in the military. "In life, you need to keep pursuing your goals and missions, and those can change at any time," he said. "But you don't give up. No matter what happens, whatever obstacles emerge, or what injuries you might sustain, or who says no to you, you have to tell yourself not to give up."

You do have to face reality. Sometimes you have to adapt and change. "You don't give up, but you do need to be willing to take your beatings and learn from them," he said. "That's what you learn as a Ranger. You can do everything right and still fail if they don't think you have what it takes. You can also make mistakes and still be successful. Don't just beat your head against the wall. Assess, adjust, and adapt. But if you give up and quit, it's just over."

Ben has spent a good portion of his career training other soldiers, and he still works as a firearms instructor. He has also invented an innovative training tool—which he calls a Dry Fire Pro Timer Training Barrel. Shooters use it to record and track pistol draw-stroke times, test carry positions, and gain other feedback so that they can develop the skills needed to get their pistols into the fight quicker.

Ben developed it and produced a prototype—no easy task. "I spent money working with someone to design the prototype, spent time and money sourcing the components in the circuitry; I had to pay money to lawyers, app developers, patent research," he said.

"It was expensive to get it to work and then to make sure it was going to keep working consistently once people bought it."

But the finished product "was such a big rush—when I finally got it to where I wanted it to be."

I understand Ben's pride. Having used the Dry Fire Pro Timer, I can vouch for its value as a training tool.

But it was not an immediate commercial success—and still isn't. "After all the work to develop it, we made a website and commercials for Instagram, and I could see that people were viewing it, but not as many of them were purchasing it as I had hoped," Ben said. "After everything I had put into it, it was devastating."

Ben wondered if he had wasted two and a half years of his life, not to mention money he could have saved for his kids' college education. But he doesn't regret the time.

"The whole process pulled me out of a funk," he said. "It was almost like being back in Ranger Battalion. There is nothing like the feeling of working on something you believe in, seeing it come together, and start to work."

Ben set a goal, believed in himself, and worked hard to accomplish his mission. As every Ranger knows, having a goal you believe in will drive you to get up every day, and from the moment you wake up until the moment you go to bed, you will be thinking, "How can I do this better, how can we make that better, or how can I be better at this?"

Despite the lackluster sales, Ben is continuing to work on the Dry Fire Pro Timer. "People who buy it like it, and hopefully there will be more of them," he said. "It's a good product.

And if it never pans out financially, it's okay. Designing it gave me an important project to pursue, and I learned so much from the process."

One of those lessons is that we are supposed to take risks. Ben thinks about the fact that modern civilization is only about 12,500 years old, and that before that time, we were all nomadic hunters and gatherers: "The people [who] survived were the people who took chances," he said.

"Until very recently, you had to hunt or fight every day just to survive. We know that character traits are passed on, and I think that the trait of risk-taking must be ingrained in all of us to some degree. It's necessary to take chances and push yourself to survive and succeed. People used to not have free time because all their time was spent pursuing their next meal. Now that we have tons of free time, we have not figured out how to use it properly or at least the healthiest way possible."

But Ben does not confuse risk with stress, and he thinks it is important to know the difference. "Enduring misery for no purpose, with no chance of reward at the end of it, that is just stress. If that's what you've got, it's okay to quit that job or make that move." Ben has defined his definition of success this way: figure out what makes you happy and don't compare yourself to other successful people.

As Rangers, Ben and I volunteered for a job that is one risk after another. We were trained to jump out of helicopters, speed down runways in the dark on motorcycles, and blow down doors.

On his first day of Ranger School, having heard all the horror stories, Ben wondered how bad it was really going to be. One guy had told him to expect that every single moment was going to be the most miserable experience of his entire life. Any moment that wasn't that bad was going to be something to enjoy.

"Like Walking into a Lion's Den"

But that is something Ben had to learn. Showing up at Ranger Battalion for the first time is intimidating, even though everyone there has signed up for it. "I was sick-to-my-stomach scared," Ben said. "It was like walking into a lion's den: I knew what was waiting for me, but I also couldn't quite imagine it yet. Even though I knew I could quit, I went in anyway. I learned that most events were not as bad as I thought they might be, and that I could survive the ones that really were bad."

Being a Ranger taught Ben to get comfortable working through fear, and it built his sense of confidence and self-respect every time he did so. "I remember being scared to the point where I almost felt sick sometimes," he said. "But I went about my business and executed my missions. I even started to enjoy that feeling. I remember the first time I got put in charge of a platoon in Ranger School, I felt like the whole world was watching and waiting for me to screw up. But I was familiar with that feeling by then, and I could say to myself, 'Okay, I'm scared, but I'm going to push past it and keep going.'"

I think that Ben gives a great explanation of how the Rangers instill the principle "Never quit."

"I Still Wanted to Do More"

In the spring of 2008, shortly after returning to Grand Junction after working as a contractor in Iraq and Africa, Ben was offered a job that would have allowed him and his family to stay in Colorado.

Ben's son and daughter had been four months old when he left them for the first time, and now they were two and a half years old.

He struggled with his decision, because he wanted to be present for his young family, but he also wanted to continue to serve his country in a meaningful way. He knew that if he and his family returned to Texas, he could go back overseas and get on a contract.

Eight months later, Ben was back in Iraq, working for the Department of State doing high-threat protection to get qualified—once again—for the CIA job. "I still wanted to do more," he said. "I truly felt as though what I had done to that point did not rise to adequately serving my country. I was starting to be in a lot of pain, but I wanted to work through it every day because I expected more of myself and felt like I owed more to my country."

Ben went back to Iraq because he felt as though many guys had given so much more than he had, and he did not feel paid up on his dues as a Ranger. I disagree with him, but I understand the way he was thinking. He was deeply frustrated to have struggled with that decision, to come so close to reaching his goal, and then have his body rebel: "Just when I finally thought that I had things figured out, the pain from my injuries got so much worse," he said. "Eventually I had to face the reality that I could not continue to perform the way I needed to for this job. I could not tough this out."

Ben says he would deploy now if he could: "I know those days are over, but I still want to fight for my country. It's not so much about our government, but for my country I would go back. Everyone in the United States has the freedom here to have a chance at a better life. I know this country has given me more chances than I deserve. I've certainly screwed up a lot of them, but I think I've finally got it right and have the life that I always wanted."

EMBRACING THE VALUES
RESPECT

Part of taking care of yourself and the people around you means that you cultivate respect in your relationships. That doesn't mean you have to like everyone or that everyone has to like you. You earn respect by making the choices that help you be the best version of yourself and by giving other people the same opportunity. Ben had the discipline to make new choices, and the courage to do it again and again until he got it right.

You might have good reasons to feel suspicious of a particular person or situation. But you can be protective and still be respectful. You don't have to be perfect, and neither does anyone else. Nobody is perfect. But you earn respect when people see you doing your best, and you feel it from yourself when you make the right choices.

Wanting to improve and working to improve represent a form of self-respect. Setting goals and meeting challenges build self-respect. Setting appropriate goals requires identifying your core values and strengths and owning them. Social media is making it difficult for many of us to be clear about our own values because we are all so busy looking for likes, taking and posting selfies, thinking about how we look, and calculating how to get attention.

Many people can't imagine life without their social media. I am challenging you right now to consider swearing off yours, at least for a little while. I no longer use Twitter. My wife, Tanya, manages my Facebook and Instagram pages, which are used for business purposes. It was uncomfortable for me to give those up at first, but I feel that having done so has helped me to take control of my time. I now spend more time with my family, more time in the gym, more time reading, more time maintaining my tactical proficiency, and more time connecting with real friends in person.

Allowing yourself to become distracted by social media can cause you to lose control of your priorities, which limits your self-respect. In addition, the way social media functions does a number on most people's self-confidence. Consider taking a break from social media and seeing how it affects your mind-set and your self-respect.

Caring for your body and your health can also be a form of self-respect. My job has required me to be physically fit and strong. It was disconcerting when I occasionally met guys in deployment situations who seemed very out of shape. They did not inspire my confidence. My physical fitness and strength have been an important part of my identity and necessary for my job.

I continue to work out every day because I like to look and feel healthy and because I know that regular exercise goes hand in hand with a positive mental state. Consider whether there are things you could do to show more respect for your physical self. In my experience, small physical improvements can lead to big positive changes in unexpected ways.

CHAPTER SIX

SELFLESS SERVICE

Put the welfare of the nation, the Army and your subordinates before your own. Selfless service is larger than just one person. In serving your country, you are doing your duty loyally without thought of recognition or gain. The basic building block of selfless service is the commitment of each team member to go a little further, endure a little longer, and look a little closer to see how he or she can add to the effort.

THE PIECE OF SCRIPTURE THAT I refer to most often is John 15:13: "Greater love hath no man than this, that a man lay down his life for his friends" (King James Version).

That means that if life is the most valuable thing that we possess, there is no greater conceivable act of love than to be willing to lay it down for friends or country.

If you are a person of faith, as I am, you know that this is what His love was and what ours should be. My parents always taught me to put the needs of other people before my own. Maybe you have seen your parents do that with your comfort or interests, or maybe you have sacrificed something for the sake of your children. I think most of us have been willing to love in this way, at least in some circumstances. Some of us are willing to take a job that requires that kind of selflessness.

There are plenty of jobs outside of the military that also

require selfless service, including those of emergency medical technicians, firefighters, police officers, and other first responders.

"Are You Willing to Give Your Life for a Stranger?"

If I were addressing a class of new recruits for any of those jobs, I would ask them: "Are you willing to give your life for a stranger on the street? Are you sure? Because this is for real. The person you might encounter who needs your help may put you in harm's way, either inadvertently or on purpose. When you intervene, when you do the job you are signing up for, there is a possibility that you might die. You need to be prepared to give your life for everyone, whether you know them or not. Whether you like them or not. Whether their reason for needing help in the first place was of their own making or not. What you are really laying down your life for is something larger: the idea of trust, of safety, of order."

If, after listening to that, someone decided to drop out, that would be a good thing. Because you need to be sure that anyone who volunteers for a job that requires selfless service will not flinch in a decisive moment. If someone is signing up for one of these jobs because they want to wear a uniform, or because they think there is going to be a good pension when they retire, they are signing up for themselves. Of course, everyone has some self-interest, but if someone is not willing to sacrifice, and they don't truly have a desire to serve, they may not truly be able to fulfill the requirements of the job when it matters most.

Selfless service, at work or at home, requires checking your ego. Selfless service requires paying attention to the needs of the people around you and committing to meet them even when doing so may cost you.

Once you make that commitment in one area, you may find that you carry it with you in all areas of your life. I know that I would lay down my life for you if you were in danger, whether I'm wearing my Ranger uniform or shorts and a Mickey Mouse T-shirt. It doesn't matter whether I am on the job. I don't care if I like you or not. Protecting and helping people is what I believe I was put on this earth to do.

SELFLESS GESTURES, LARGE AND SMALL

On the night of September 11, 2012, our team in Benghazi was not required to go out to defend the ambassador's compound, but there was no debate about it. When we heard the radio call, "GRS, we need you," everyone's attitude was, "Hell yes, we're going."

Protecting Americans was our job, and we were going to do it. I had no special relationship with the CIA staff. Americans were under attack. They were scared and outnumbered, and they didn't know what to do.

Our team *did* know what to do. We got our gear and we went out to fight. If anyone was worried for his own life or wondering about the legal or financial ramifications if one of us got wounded, he never mentioned it.

It was selfless service for Glen Doherty to get that jet to us in Benghazi when we had no other air support. I'm sure Glen didn't even think about whether he was going to live or die. He and his team did the right thing, even though they had to go through private channels to arrange it and they put themselves in harm's way. For us.

Mark "Oz" Geist and Dave Ubben, a State Department security agent, were seriously wounded and might have bled out if that jet hadn't been there to fly them to a place where they could get proper medical treatment. Glen's selfless service saved their lives.

There was a lot of selfless service in that battle. Rone and Jack and Tig went into the ambassador's villa over and over again, plunging into thick clouds of smoke to try to find the ambassador and locate survivors. It is disorienting to fight through smoke: it burns your eyes, it clouds your vision, it compromises your breathing, and it makes you feel as if you are going to pass out. It was an act of selfless service for them to subject themselves to those conditions in order to find others.

It is selfless service for soldiers to remain in their fighting positions instead of running and hiding whenever shooting starts. In Benghazi, the enemy continued to fire after the mortars hit us. If we had all taken cover, the militia could have approached our compound using small-arms fire, and if they had gotten inside, we would have been screwed. That didn't happen because everyone stayed on our rooftop positions and continued to fight, not knowing if we were going to get mortared again.

Our night of fighting in Benghazi was full of dramatic examples of selfless service, but the truth is that selflessness is a quality that is required even in times of peace. A peaceful, civil society is held up by thousands of small gestures of ordinary selflessness.

In Chapter Five, "Respect", I mentioned the high level of mistrust that some people had in Iraq, and I described how I used to try to remind guys who were suspicious that not all locals were terrorists. Most locals were just trying to live their lives. It made sense if the locals seemed frustrated with us, because we were disrupting their lives. Just imagine trying to drive to work in the morning on your regular route and, all of a sudden, you run into a huge motorcade blocking the road. Today it is going to take you two hours to get to work instead of your standard twenty minutes. Wouldn't you be pissed off? That is one of the more benign ways that we were turning their lives upside down. It is unsurprising that some of the locals would disdain Americans.

I still had to do my job, but my awareness of how my activity was affecting others helped me to display patience, understanding, and respect in circumstances when it would have been easy, and understandable, to just respond to negativity in kind.

Sometimes it was challenging to distinguish an actual bad guy from a good guy who was just having a bad day. Sometimes I encountered an angry guy, sitting in traffic, trying to get home, and getting frustrated.

During my time in Iraq in 2004 and 2005, I was rarely in my best state of mind. It was often 120 degrees in the shade and I was constantly at risk of being hit by a sniper's bullet or a grenade, especially when I was working. And my work entailed being primarily responsible for safeguarding someone else's security. When I am in that state of mind and I intersect with a guy experiencing a case of road rage, I can see that there is a tremendous amount of tension in that moment.

It is a kind of service to be able to take a deep breath and smile, or to make a friendly or respectful hand gesture, or to make an effort to communicate in the local language. When we were able not only to do our jobs, but to work in a respectful way that built trust and goodwill, that was a different kind of selfless service.

ISRAEL MATOS

Sergeant Israel Matos, USMC, Retired, is a firearms trainer who runs Operation Veteran Outdoors (OVO). This nonprofit creates recreational opportunities for veterans who have been wounded in combat, connects them with services if they need them, and gives them a chance to spend time with other veterans who understand what they are going through. Israel understands just how tough the transition back into civilian life can be: he joined the Marine Corps out of high school. Being a Marine was the only job Israel had ever known before he was wounded in Afghanistan in 2011 by an enemy using a donkey carrying sixty to eighty pounds of explosives.

"The only thing I regret is that I'm not still in active service," he told me years later. But wait, I'm getting ahead of myself.

Israel hadn't been sure exactly how he would serve in the military, but he never seriously considered another line of work. "Our dad had served in the Army, although he didn't talk about it a lot, and never pushed me to join," he said. "My mom wasn't in the military, but she could scare a military instructor, so I feel like she did her part to help prepare me."

Israel grew up in the Spanish Harlem section of New York City in a four-bedroom apartment. Israel's parents had four biological children and fostered sixteen children, three of whom they adopted, including Israel. "I was a quiet kid, and I always wanted to help people," he told me.

Israel said he was a happy kid, but he always knew he didn't want to stay in the big city. As a child, he joined the Civil Air Patrol's Cadet Program. During his time with the patrol, Israel learned about aviation and got exposed to a military model of organization; it made an impression.

Throughout Israel's childhood, his father served as a member of the Army Reserves, which influenced Israel's decision to join the military.

"I Wanted to Help"

In 2001, Israel's father—still in the Army Reserves—took Israel with him to work at an armory in Manhattan. "Watching him and seeing what he did with the Reserves just reinforced that I wanted to help," he recalled. "I wanted to be a part of that."

Israel's father had absorbed lessons from his own military service that he passed on to Israel. "When I was fourteen, I was late for a Civil Air Patrol meeting and my uniform was a mess," he recalled. "My dad stopped me as I was running out the door and told me to stand at attention. My dad took out a Polaroid camera and took a picture of me. Then he sent me back to iron the shirt and get dressed again, and then he took another picture. He held both pictures up and asked me, 'Which one of these guys would you want to call for help? Which one looks like he has his act together?' I always remember that."

Israel's father was helpful to others in his neighborhood as well, and his example was a powerful influence on Israel.

"My dad always reached out, even when he couldn't really afford it, and I saw how loved he was in the community;

people still respect him when he walks into a room," Israel said.

"Even in our family, people know that they can turn to him when the chips are down, and, to me, that is worth a lot. It is basic to my understanding of what it means to live a good life. I didn't want to be just another homeboy back on the block. I wanted to be independent, to contribute, and to be respected like my father."

Israel's older brother had already joined the infantry by the time Israel graduated from high school. Between his father and his brother and the Civil Air Patrol, Israel felt like he knew what he was getting into when he joined the Marines.

But as prepared as Israel was for military service, he said that he found Marine Corps boot camp to be "a brain reset."

Israel was as happy as he had ever been at Camp Geiger in North Carolina, but was humbled by the challenge of it. The expectations were high, and Israel's confidence continued to grow as he met the challenges. He was stimulated by the skills he was learning.

"The great thing about the Marine Corps is the way they cross-train people," he said. "Sometimes I think people don't realize everything we do and have to know as infantrymen: maps, medical training, construction, demolition, conflict de-escalation, foreign languages, ridiculous amounts of math, and you are constantly pushed to be the best at everything, because it will be your life on the line, and the lives of your fellow Marines on the line."

After three months in the School of Infantry, Israel qualified as an infantry assaultman, or "51" as they are sometimes called, because the specialty is number 0351 in the Military Occupational Specialties list.

"Ready for Anything"

"We used to carry the demolition packs and Mk 153 SMAW," he said, referring to the Mark 153 shoulder-launched multipurpose assault weapon. "But we had to be ready for anything."

Israel turned eighteen when he got to his unit, 2/2 Echo Company, a helicopter company, and then he moved to 2/2 Fox Company, an amphibious company, a move that proved easy because they were based in Camp Lejeune, right up the road.

Israel's first experiences overseas involved delivering food, setting up hospitals, and training local military units. "It felt like I was finally doing something and truly helping others," he said. "I was also getting to see the world. I was in Italy, Spain, the Seychelles, Kenya." Israel loved the feeling of seeing an immediate result after they completed a mission.

"A Good Reset" in the United States

In 2007, Israel went to Iraq for the first time. "It was a good experience, but that kind of deployment was naturally more stressful because it was a lot of convoys and standing posts and I was worried about every crack I stepped on," he said. "In some ways, I would almost rather be in a firefight compared with our routines in Iraq. At least a battle would be head-on, rather than looking over my shoulder every minute and wondering when something would happen."

During this deployment, Israel faced another source of tension: it was difficult for him to see his girlfriend, Terisa (who would become his wife a year later). He started to think about finding a job Stateside.

After completing his deployment in 2008, Israel reenlisted

as a firearms instructor at a rifle range. From 2008 to 2010, he was based in Quantico, Virginia, where he helped establish the Marine Corps Combat Pistol Program.

Israel initially thought that he wanted to work his way toward joining a shooting team, but he performed well as an instructor and was encouraged to continue. "It got to the point where, if someone was really struggling, it'd be, 'Send him to Izzy,'" he said. "I didn't mind. I like helping people. And it's important to get it right. Hell, the lieutenant you're training could wind up being the commander."

Having seen Israel teach, I imagine he was outstanding. He has the knowledge and quiet authority that an effective instructor needs, but he is also funny and he puts people at ease.

Israel is fluent in Spanish and English, so he was assigned to work with officers from the Mexican marine corps for a while, doing firearms training. Israel and Terisa, who had met as teenagers in church, were married in 2009. Israel's life seemed to be settling into a productive, peaceful routine. "I made good friends," he said. "My buddy, Travis Bankston, who I met in Virginia, is still the only person I let touch my guns and is one of the few people I trust. Being in the United States for a while was a good reset."

I understand what he means. When I am deploying, I am on edge in a way that I never am at home. I'm not unhappy overseas, but I have to maintain a level of situational awareness that can wear on me over time.

"Back in the Fight"

In 2010, Israel got a call from Chris Champion, a Marine in 2/2 Fox Company. A friend of Israel, another Marine, had been killed by an improvised explosive device (IED) in Afghanistan. Israel was already up for new orders, and he immediately requested orders to go overseas. "I wanted to be back in the fight—to hell with my career," he recalled. "I know that the work I was doing in Virginia was helping, indirectly, but I really wanted to get back to my job as a Marine. I thought that I could help, and I just wanted to be back in the heart of it."

On December 30, 2010, Israel joined his brothers at the Marine Corps Air Ground Combat Center in Twentynine Palms, in southern San Bernardino, California.

He was assigned to 3rd Battalion, 4th Marines, which was nicknamed Darkside. "I spent three months training with the platoon, and then we went into combat together in March," Israel said.

Israel's platoon was based in the Upper Gereshk Valley in Afghanistan's notorious Helmand Province. They were tasked with maintaining control of the valley. It was dangerous work. "We were basically static security, and the enemy had figured out that there's no real beating us in a gunfight, so they were constantly monitoring us and trying to figure out our schedules and then ambush us," he said. "Between those efforts and the IEDs, I think we probably had at least one injury or casualty from our battalion every three days."

So many people were getting hit that Israel's platoon was replacing squads and rotating guys in and out frequently; he felt like there were always new people to get to know.

"The conditions we were living in were tough," Israel said. "It was incredibly hot, and we were more or less living in holes in the ground or mud huts."

The unit did what they could to alleviate the tension. "The

Platoon Commander, Lieutenant Anthony, he was just five-six, but he was a powerhouse," Israel said. "He helped turn this one pit in the ground into a little lodge with camp netting, a place to work out, or to hang out, even to barbecue sometimes.

"At first, people were skeptical about his vision, but by the time it was done, everyone loved it. It sounds crazy, but it helped people. We were living in tough conditions, and we needed everyone to be at 100 percent physically and mentally, so even a little makeshift patio that helped people relax meant something."

That relaxation didn't last. June 15, 2011, should have been a routine day, but conditions felt off right from the start. Israel was on the entry control point from seven to ten in the morning, which was normally the busiest time of the day. "But that day, there was nothing going on. It was weirdly quiet."

A boy on a moped approached a bridge checkpoint, where Marines stopped and searched him, which was their usual practice there.

The boy was carrying nothing but a new cell phone. In retrospect, Israel said, that should have made him suspicious. "But I said, 'Let him go; he has nothing we can use to hold him,'" he told me.

The teenager drove off, stopped after about four or five hundred yards, and then just sat on his moped behind a brick wall. The team had eyes on him, but they were not alarmed.

The team was about twenty minutes from the patrol base, and they had taken a few potshots from the tree line the prior evening, but it had otherwise been uneventful.

"Then a younger kid, maybe nine years old, emerges on the road," Israel recalled. "He was walking and leading a donkey with a pack on his back. Our guys tried to stop and check him, but there was nothing in the pack of the donkey. But that donkey was moving like he was carrying a lot of weight."

Israel was talking to Doc, a Navy corpsman, at the entry control point, and observing the interactions at the bridge crossing. "Doc and I were talking about our families, but I was watching as the kid walked up, and paying attention to the way the donkey moved." Israel remembered having an uneasy feeling. "I'm not sure how to make sense of it, but something was clearly telling me that something was bad."

The interpreter was walking toward the boy with the donkey to get more information when Israel stepped forward to pull the interpreter back, telling everyone "to duck, to get back, to get down, to get the fuck out of the way." Israel was about twenty feet away from what investigators later determined to be sixty to eighty pounds of explosives as they detonated. It wasn't possible to determine, later, where the donkey had been carrying the explosives, but it was clear that there had been a relationship between the explosion and the young man on the moped waiting by the wall. The certificate from Israel's Corps Commendation Medal from the Navy notes, "After recognizing an enemy on a motorcycle was acting as a decoy to expose the search team to the blast, Sergeant Matos ordered his Marines to take cover in the search area bunker. With disregard for his own safety, he placed himself at the entrance of the search area and physically threw Marines into the covered area as the detonation occurred...He saved the lives of the Marines in his search team."

Israel's body took most of the shrapnel from the explosion. His right knee, tibia, calf, and patella were torn up. "My leg was smashed, I knew that, but I don't remember a lot from the moment of impact," he said. "I've seen video of someone patching my wounds later. Seeing it was really something, way different from going through it."

Israel, who was conscious immediately after the explosion, remembered thinking, "Shit, I need a corpsman," but also, "Is everyone else all right?"

Israel was taken by helicopter to the local hospital. "When I was on the bird, there were times that I was completely conscious, but I was confused, and I looked at the guys, who were all geared up, and wondered, 'Who are these bug eyes?'" he recalled. "I don't know if I tried to talk to them, but they can only give you a thumbs-up or a thumbs-down anyway because it's so loud."

"Everything Went Black"

While on the helicopter, some of Israel's patching came undone and he started to bleed out. One of his fellow Marines moved in quickly to revive him: "I woke up and there was this big, bug-eyed dude rubbing the shit on my chest to get me to respond, and then everything went black."

Israel woke up in the hospital. Feeling nothing, he thought, "Am I dead?" The lights in the room were bright, and Israel could hear voices speaking local Afghani dialect in the background. Israel realized that a woman was nearby, and he tried to ask her if he was dead. She answered, in a British accent, "Hey, Marine."

Israel described this first moment of consciousness as surreal: "I thought I might be dead since I went from having so much pain to feeling nothing at all. I remember thinking that I wanted to get the attention of the nurse, but I couldn't lift my arm. I couldn't feel anything at all. When I took my first real, conscious breath, I had a feeling I had never experienced before. As that breath came into my lungs, it felt like my chest was on fire, but there was no pain, only a feeling of euphoria, and it radiated through my entire body, flooding me. I have never experienced anything like that before or since."

Israel wanted to know if he had gotten all his guys home. He had. He called Terisa. "I told her I was so sorry," he recalled. "I always promised that I would come home in one piece. I told her I got hit, but I didn't want to tell her what had happened."

The doctors wanted to amputate Israel's leg. "They were talking amputation on the first day," Israel recalled, but he told one doctor, "Dude, I've grown attached to that thing over the past twenty-five years."

Israel didn't want anyone to see him in his wounded state, especially his family, but his older brother happened to be working as a coordinator for the Wounded Warrior Regiment at the time of the explosion and he was able to see Israel's medical reports and monitor his progress from the United States.

He arranged for Israel's family to see him when he stopped at Andrews Air Force Base on the way to Balboa Naval Medical Center in San Diego. "I remember my mom was crying and my dad was shaking his head, 'You couldn't just be a helicopter pilot?'"

At the hospital in San Diego, Terisa was waiting for him. Israel recalled, "It seemed like a dozen doctors were all standing there as I arrived, asking a million questions, and I just remember that all I wanted to do was be alone with my wife and hold her in my arms."

Israel was not only struggling physically, but mentally: "I was a Marine, and, at that point, I couldn't bend over to pick things up or turn to wipe my own ass. It was depressing, and the reality of my situation was starting to sink in now that I had made it back home."

Israel's leg wounds left him highly susceptible to infection, and he underwent surgery the day he arrived in San Diego. It was the first of what would be twenty-two surgeries, many of which involved the removal of diseased tissue and muscle from his leg, which was rebuilt with cadaver parts.

That leg is now an inch and a half shorter than the other and has a ten-degree bow, but he still has it.

By the summer of 2011, Israel was in rehab, trying to walk without crutches or a cane. It was painful just to stand up.

"I was able to stand up on one leg, but when the blood would rush into my leg it would feel as though my leg was going to explode," he said.

Israel, used to acting like a badass, was trying to hide his pain and his limp. "I really wanted to get back to work," he said, "They tried giving me a few different assignments—I went to Coronado to help with teaching; I taught at a rifle range in Pensacola—but after a week or two of walking at full speed, my cadaver parts would break down or get infected and then I'd be down for the count for three more weeks recovering from another surgery."

Israel was medically retired from the Marine Corps on December 31, 2013. He was twenty-seven years old. "I wanted to work, but I just kept breaking down. I knew I couldn't do what an infantryman needs to do anymore, like put on a 120-pound pack, hike up a mountain, and fight."

Israel felt supported by the Marine Corps as he tried to figure out his next move: "The Marines kept me in for two years after my injuries, through all the surgeries. They gave me a lot of opportunities to retrain and continue to be of service by helping in other ways, like at the armory. I gave it my all, but my leg kept breaking."

Israel had been a Marine for his entire adult life. He had no idea what to do next.

"I loved being a Marine and I really tried to stay," he said. "I was on my eighteenth surgery by the time I got out."

Israel was in California when he left the military, and he and Terisa packed up their car and drove across the country to stay with family in New Jersey.

"Essentially Homeless"

"Once you get out, you're kind of on your own—at least that's how it felt at the time," Israel said. "My wife and I were essentially homeless for about three months. We were living in Terisa's grandparents' garage and trying to make a plan."

The couple had been on the East Coast for about six months when an organization called the Military Warriors Support Foundation, in conjunction with Bank of America, offered to move them into a house in Palm Bay, Florida, in 2014. "We were so grateful," he said.

Israel ultimately wound up receiving support from some great organizations and people, which is part of what motivates him to work today with Operation Veteran Outdoors. "Semper Fi Fund, Homes for Heroes, and the Military Warriors Support Foundation all helped me to get it together and figure out a new life," he said. "I definitely needed guidance."

When Israel and Terisa moved into their new house, the Military Warriors Support Foundation held a ceremony at which a man approached Israel and said, "You don't know me from a hole in the wall, but just know I've got your back."

That made Israel uncomfortable: "I thought it was a little strange, honestly, like, 'You don't know me; why would you have my back?' I guess I tend to be suspicious of people."

That man was named Bill Orndorf, and Bill would come to play a vital role in Israel's recovery.

It was the rainy season in Florida, and right after they moved in to their house Israel and his wife found a hole in the roof. "We were very grateful to have our house, but the weather was challenging and it exposed a few kinks in the house that needed to get fixed," Israel said.

"I started to get stressed out. We had only been there a week, so I didn't have a job yet. I remember thinking, 'I've got to get a job and make money so that we can fix all this stuff right away.' In the meantime, my wife messaged this guy, Bill, from the party, basically a random stranger we've met once, and said, 'We need your help.' "

At first, Israel was angry that Terisa had reached out for help to someone they didn't know. Now he's grateful.

"No joke, within twenty minutes of Terisa making that call, I was getting messages from contractors, water people, an AC guy, and a plumber, all wanting to schedule time to come over and fix the house," Israel said. "Forty minutes later, a truck full of filtered water shows up for us to use. Maybe two hours after that, I get a call from Bill himself. He said, 'Hey, I'm going to a range. Do you want to come shoot with me?' "

Israel wasn't going to say no after all the goodwill that had just come his way. "We got to talking and shooting and we just hit it off," Israel recalled. "Bill was a finance guy. He had been a senior vice president at Merrill Lynch, and he had made it his mission to help veterans. Bill is a pretty tough dude himself. He took me under his wing and helped me learn to be a productive civilian."

Doctors had been straightforward with Israel about the problems associated with having a limb salvage, and Israel has struggled with most of them. Israel's twenty-two surgeries have all been from the hip down. "Something is always happening and I need to change something out like at a Jiffy Lube," he said. "Hardware breaks, or I need new screws, or one of the cadaver bones breaks and needs to be replaced, or the soft tissue becomes infected."

Israel jokes about it, but he has been in constant pain since the explosion. He could use a knee replacement, but doctors have told him that he only has enough live bone to do one knee replacement in his lifetime, and since they last from ten to twenty years and Israel is still a young man, he is trying to delay having that done for as long as possible.

"It Is Not an Easy Life"

"There were a lot of casualties in Afghanistan in 2011, so I actually knew a lot of other Marines with limb salvages out of the same facility in San Diego that I was in, and a good amount of them have either chosen to amputate or have since committed suicide," Israel said. "It is not an easy life."

But Israel still feels the work to rebuild his leg has been worth it. "I love to drive, and I still want to fly," he said. "It has been the right thing for me to keep this leg, so far, because of the things I want to do."

And Israel has never stopped training. Between 2011 and 2013, he learned how to walk again—and how to shoot again.

In 2012, Israel met Dave Bridgeman, a competitive shooter, at a shooting event for wounded veterans outside of San Diego hosted by the Semper Fi Fund, a nonprofit organization that provides programs to assist wounded veterans.

"Dave invited me to a United States Practical Shooting Association competition," Israel recalled. "I was still on crutches and I still had an X-fix, like a giant metal cage stabilizer, on my leg, but I was so motivated to get back to business, I would drive one and a half hours to get to these private matches."

The practical shooting appealed to Israel's sense of mission. "When I maintain these skills, then I feel that I am still an asset in some way," he said. "No one is going to break into my house and rob me, and I can help other people have that same confidence about their skills."

Israel is still working on his childhood goal of becoming a commercial licensed helicopter pilot. "Working toward it on my own definitely wasn't my plan, and my mom still gets upset when she thinks about it because she doesn't want me to do anything dangerous anymore," he said.

But noting that his passion for flying dates back to his days in the Civil Air Patrol as a teenager, he feels that the lessons have been worth the effort and expense: "Pursuing the license has been an important way to motivate myself. Shooting and flying both remind me of who I am."

If you were to meet Israel on the street today, you wouldn't necessarily know that he had sustained a life-altering injury. He can't run, and he walks slowly, but he moves with purpose and chooses whether to share his story.

"I'll talk about it if someone asks me, but people don't always put it together," he said. "I think I hide it well."

Israel credits his Marine training for his ability to push through pain and deal with it matter-of-factly. "I remember once, in training, coming back from a twenty-six-mile hike after a week in the field," he said. "I had walked until the soles of my feet had worn away, literally, so I was kind of hopping and wincing as I was walking on the catwalk in my shower shoes back to my room in the barracks, because it felt like walking on hot coals."

A lance corporal, Israel recalled, "stopped me as I walked by his room and said, 'We're Marines. Stop being a pussy and stow that shit.'"

Though Israel does not think that everyone dealing with pain has to be a stoic, he does think that everyone needs to set goals.

"When you stay focused on a goal, it gives you something to wake up to other than pain," he said.

He also thinks that serving others has been key to his own recovery and his ability to maintain a positive attitude. Israel works as a shooting instructor and runs a website, shooting-classes.com, which connects students with instructors.

He also serves as president of Operation Veteran Outdoors, which provides recreational opportunities to Purple Heart recipients and other combat veterans. OVO organizes events at which veterans with similar injuries and experiences interact with one another and get information about other programs and services that may help them in their transitions back to civilian life.

"A great weekend for me is taking veterans out hunting, even though I'm not a hunter, or volunteering at a soup kitchen," said Israel, whose position at OVO is a volunteer one. "Sometimes getting out of your own head and feeling like you are of service to others is the best medicine."

I have watched Israel on the range, and I think that his ability to make people smile represents another kind of service that he is providing.

"We are teaching serious stuff, but I want people to be comfortable," he said.

Israel also attended classes sponsored by Semper Fi in San Diego, where he learned and took to heart the acronym VAULT: valued, accepted, understood, loved, and trusted.

"That is my benchmark when I'm working with people, especially with OVO," he said. "I want you to feel those things when you are with me, and when you are among your fellow warriors. I don't care, I'll start floss dancing with my full gun belt on if it breaks the ice."

Israel's relentlessly positive attitude belies his chronic pain. Some mornings, "I wake up and my muscles have contracted overnight in a cramp, and I have to massage it and stretch it out slowly just to stand up," he said.

"Sometimes I can kind of get the muscles firing again by forcing my brace on, but however it resolves, that is how my day starts at least once a week."

Israel also has tinnitus, the perception of a constant ringing sound: "The worst times of the day are when I'm waking up and falling asleep," he said.

But Israel believes that, veteran or not, everyone has to identify their problems and tackle them, one step at a time: "If something is bothering me when I wake up, I remind myself that I've got stuff to do, and that I've got people counting on me. That works for me because I never want to let anyone down. Someone else might need to tell themselves something different, but I'm motivated by people counting on me."

"Check Your Ego at the Door"

Israel thinks that most service members are motivated, at least in part, by altruism. "If you are going to be successful in the military, you do need to check your ego at the door," he said. "You are volunteering to be in some challenging situations, usually because someone else's life is on the line. You are signing a check—up to and including your own life and everything in between. There is an old saying that the military makes bad men worse and good men better, and I think that is true. If someone is just trying to use the military strictly to get something out of it personally, those are the people who tend to come out angry and disappointed, because it does require sacrifice."

He credited a sense of patriotism as an important factor in his decision to join the Marines. "I still get choked up hearing 'The Star-Spangled Banner' and seeing fireworks on the Fourth of July," he said. "The United States is a special place, a free place, and I think most people have a sense of wanting to protect this land, even thinking of this as a larger family. That's how I think about it. I always felt like I was protecting something valuable."

But he acknowledged that the transition to civilian life can be tough for many veterans, even those who were not wounded. "To go from a regimented life, where someone else is making all your decisions and choices, to being out in the civilian world, is an overwhelming change," he said.

Israel had joined the Marines at age seventeen and hadn't known any other kind of life as an adult when he left the service. "I had a lot of insecurity when I came out," he recalled. "I didn't have anyone to protect; I didn't know what my mission was anymore. It was disorienting, and then I had all the physical injuries on top of it."

He noted that people who commit to military service are committing to a disciplined mind-set. "Some of it is painful, and you are going to miss out on things, but I don't know if everyone figures that out until they are home and it's over, and that can be a reckoning."

Israel reflected on other men his age and thought about how their lives compared with his own and those of his fellow warriors: "Some of us were at war while everyone else was at home, walking around a mall or drinking at bars. It was interesting to get out and realize that, in some ways, I was more mature than my peers, because of what I had been through, but in other ways, I was very immature. For example, my life had been so rigid and structured, I felt awkward in the social ways of civilian life. I had to get comfortable interacting with people."

"They Have No Idea What Veterans Have Been Through"

Israel found that there were some things that those civilians just didn't understand. "I remember, when I first came back, being at a big group dinner in a Ruby Tuesday and someone asked me what it was like to be in a gunfight. I remember thinking, 'Why would you ask me that at dinner, in front of kids?' It is a reminder that many civilians might appreciate us, but they have no idea what veterans have been through."

Years after he left the military, Israel is still a warrior. "Being a Marine helps me push, because I don't want to fail and I don't want to quit because that isn't what Marines do," he said. "I still have a mission. It is to try to help other people."

Trying to continue to carry out that mission has been the key to Israel's recovery and is his best advice for other people who are facing adversity: "Find something that you know you are good at it and use that skill to connect with other people and to help as many people as you can. I don't care if it's underwater basket weaving. Reintegrating is hard. It is tempting to shut yourself off because you don't want people to see you struggle or be in pain. But if you can find something that motivates you to stay connected and help as many people as you can, you'll feel a sense of purpose."

EMBRACING THE VALUES
SELFLESS SERVICE

Anyone who serves in the military, and anyone who is willing to put him or herself at risk as a first responder, is offering the ultimate selfless service. When you volunteer for that kind of job, you are willing to lay down your life for someone else. Thousands of people risk their lives every day just by going to work, and I'm afraid that too many of us take for granted their bravery, and the courage and sacrifice of their loved ones.

Our communities' ability to function depends on the willingness of significant numbers of people to volunteer for dangerous service. The security of our nation depends on the people who are willing to go into battle to fight for it. The safety of other nations is also dependent on American troops, because we are still the very best in the world at what we do. Some of the men and women who sign up for that work do sacrifice their lives, and many others return home and live and work among us without broadcasting what they have given up or how the consequences of their selfless service shape their lives today.

Take a moment to think about how you express your appreciation for the sacrifices that the men and women on the front lines make for all of us. If you are not satisfied with what you are doing, identify an action you will take in the coming weeks or months that will align with your level of gratitude.

Now, think about the ways that you offer selfless service in your own life. You probably already do that to some degree, even if you don't literally put your life on the line. There are many practical ways in which we put other people's needs before our own, often for our children or for our good friends. But have you ever sacrificed something in order to protect or improve your neighborhood? Your community institutions? Your town? Your state? It could be time, money, or other resources. Giving any of those can be a kind of selfless service. Think how much stronger our country could be if we each expanded the network of people to whom we offer our selfless service.

It may sound counterintuitive, but selfless service also helps the people who provide it. People don't perform truly selfless service for their own benefit, but that is often a happy result. I think Israel's recovery illustrates how powerful it can be to give of yourself.

Feelings of satisfaction and peace come from helping others and offering yourself up, whether to a team, an organization, or your country; your service will make you more connected to other people who are part of the same community. As the community of people that you serve expands, the web of connections that you create will grow more complex, and the impact of your service may be more profound than you imagined possible.

CHAPTER SEVEN

HONOR

Live up to Army values. The nation's highest military award is The Medal of Honor. This award goes to Soldiers who make honor a matter of daily living—Soldiers who develop the habit of being honorable, and solidify that habit with every value choice they make. Honor is a matter of carrying out, acting, and living the values of respect, duty, loyalty, selfless service, integrity and personal courage in everything you do.

THERE ARE SO MANY STORIES of bravery and heroism on the battlefield that are forgotten, even ones that are relatively recent. It is our patriotic duty to try to document and honor the sacrifices that are made by the men and women who fight for our country. The military has procedures and memorials to preserve and commemorate the heroic acts of soldiers who are wounded or die in combat while going above and beyond the call of duty. These awards and designations serve as a guide to help future generations understand our history and our values, so it is important to understand whom we choose to honor and for what.

The Medal of Honor is the highest award for combat valor that a soldier can earn, and the only one that must be approved by the president of the United States. It has been awarded over 3,400 times since it was created in 1861 and, as of this writing, only twenty-five times since Vietnam. The Medal of Honor requires more than just selfless service or even extraordinary courage under fire. It requires "incontestable proof of the performance of meritorious conduct" that must "involve great personal bravery or self-sacrifice so conspicuous as to clearly distinguish the individual above his or her comrades and must have involved risk of life."

ALWYN CASHE

I can't think of anyone who illustrates the principles of honor and selfless service more than Army Sergeant First Class Alwyn C. "Al" Cashe. He was a tough noncommissioned officer and master gunner from Sanford, Florida, who joined the Army after graduating from Oviedo High School in 1988.

Cashe was thirty-five years old and on his second deployment to Iraq in the province of Salahuddin, running a routine patrol on October 17, 2005, when an IED detonated next to his Bradley fighting vehicle, called Alpha 13. The Bradley rolled to a stop, already engulfed in flames, when the enemy began to fire. The ammunition on Alpha 13 ignited, but Alpha 12, the Bradley behind them, began returning fire on the insurgents.

A Bradley is a hulking, powerful machine. The way the Bradley is structured, it's hard to get out of it if the vehicle is on fire or in water. The Bradley is a mechanized armored infantry fighting vehicle equipped with a twenty-five-millimeter cannon and multiple antitank TOW (tube-launched, optically tracked, wire-guided) missiles.

It holds three crew members up top or in front to drive it and control the weapons systems; an infantry squad of six or nine soldiers can ride in the back. Soldiers can fight from inside a Bradley using modified M16 rifles mounted in firing ports, or they can lower a platform to exit the vehicle and move or fight on foot.

The explosion that ignited the fuel cell in Alpha 13 killed the team's interpreter immediately. Cashe was in the gun turret of the vehicle at the moment of the explosion and initially sustained only minor wounds. Witnesses say that Cashe and Sergeant Daniel Connelly climbed down into the hull of the vehicle and pulled out the driver, Specialist Darren Howe, who was on fire. They put that fire out, and then Connelly stayed with Howe while Cashe returned to Alpha 13. The uniform that Cashe was wearing was soaked with fuel from the explosion, and as he returned to Alpha 13, he caught on fire.

The soldiers managed to lower the ramp to the payload compartment, where the rest of the crew was caught inside the raging blaze. Cashe returned to the burning Bradley vehicle three times while he himself was on fire and got the interpreter and every one of his soldiers out, all while under enemy fire.

I've never been on fire, but I have run into it, and the idea that Cashe returned *three times* into the choking smoke and heat of a blazing Bradley while his own body was in flames humbles and amazes me. In the end, Cashe was the most severely wounded man on the scene, with three-quarters of his body covered in second- and third-degree burns.

Last Man On, Last Man Out

When a medevac bird was finally able to land near the scene, Cashe insisted on being the last man on. He waited, according to witnesses, until every one of his guys had been loaded onto the helicopters, and then he refused to be carried to the medevac on a stretcher. Guys on the scene say that Cashe's uniform was burned and his skin was smoldering. Cashe accepted some assistance, but he walked onto that bird on his own two feet. Accounts from the scene say that his boots, helmet, and body armor were the only intact things left on him.

Cashe was conscious when he arrived at the US Air Force Theater Hospital at Balad Air Base in Iraq, and the medics who treated him there recall him asking only about everyone else, despite his own severe injuries. The translator had been killed in action and ten soldiers were injured, seven of them very seriously. Cashe's own injuries were the worst of the group. All of the wounded were taken to Brooke Army Medical Center in San Antonio, Texas, where three other soldiers died from their burns. In the same way that he had been the last man to board the medevac bird, Cashe was the last man out. He died on November 8, 2005.

Cashe was posthumously awarded the Silver Star, the Army's third-highest honor. Major General Gary M. Brito, who recommended Cashe for the Silver Star, concluded, after additional review of Cashe's conduct, that he should be awarded the Medal of Honor. Brito submitted Cashe's nomination to the Army in May 2011. If the campaign is successful, Cashe may become the first African American soldier among the post-9/11 warriors to receive the Medal of Honor.

If Cashe doesn't meet the qualifications for a Medal of Honor, I don't know who could. His Silver Star citation directly credits him with saving the lives of six soldiers. A lot of other people feel the same way. A retired Cold War–era veteran named Harry Conner created a campaign to upgrade

Cashe's Silver Star. Like Cashe, Conner served with the 3rd Infantry. He has bicycled over 1,700 miles and started a Facebook page to publicize the story of Cashe's bravery and the efforts to award him the Medal of Honor.

"No one deserves the Medal of Honor more," said Jimmy Ryan, who met Cashe at Fort Benning, Georgia, in 2004, when Ryan was a lieutenant and Cashe was a platoon sergeant. But, he added, Cashe himself was not motivated by dreams of glory. "Al wouldn't care about any of this," he said.

Both men were there to serve in a mechanized unit, the 3rd Brigade, 3rd Infantry Division. They spent nine months at Fort Benning, gearing up to deploy to Iraq. "There was something very tough about Al," Ryan said. "He was not a huge guy, but he had not an ounce of body fat and was extremely strong. He was also extremely knowledgeable."

Ryan was already an experienced Ranger when he met Cashe. Ryan had enlisted in the Army in 1991, but he graduated from Officer Candidate School in 2003. He asked to be assigned to a mechanized unit because, until then, his career had been with light units or special ops.

"Al knew way more than I did," Ryan recalled. "A unit had just gotten back from Iraq, and there was downsizing when they returned. We had to rebuild the platoon and start training hard, getting proficient with our weapons systems as a team, and studying, trying to learn from what was happening in Iraq on the ground. Al shot the best out of the entire brigade in one of the live-fire preparations. He was very good at what he did."

Cashe and Ryan deployed to Iraq in January of 2005. "It was an ass-kicker," Ryan told me. "The heat was relentless. Our living arrangements were not great. We were living outside the city of Samarra in these metal structures kind of like cans that were about eight by fifteen feet."

Ryan had deployed previously to southern Africa, but this was his first combat deployment. Ryan would go on to serve two long deployments in Afghanistan, but this period in Iraq stands out for him. "Sometimes we found bombs three times in one day," Ryan said. "We would have a mission and a strategy every morning, but then when we found a bomb, we would have to stop to deal with that and it would slow our momentum."

A lot of the locals in the area they were patrolling had been hard-core loyalists to President Saddam Hussein, who had been deposed by a US-led coalition in 2003. "We tried hard to build a lot of trust and faith in the population," Ryan said. "We were just trying to get things functioning properly. We connected with the schools, and with different projects for water and for electricity."

But their job was tough because the security situation on the ground had fallen apart in many ways. "When we first got there, there were local police and local army units, but they were in disarray after the invasion," Ryan said. "Sometimes it felt like anarchy. There was looting and other criminal activity. We had to address that and search vehicles, yards, and homes. We got into some pretty good fights, and then, after I left in May, things got really hostile."

As uncomfortable as it got, "I felt proud of what we were doing," Ryan said. "At the micro level, I know we helped a lot of people. When you are working in a situation like that, where there are so many needs, you have a powerful sense of belonging and purpose."

Cashe and Ryan were in charge of fifty-four soldiers. "It

was an awesome group of guys, and Al was an old-school leader," Ryan told me. "He was extremely knowledgeable, and when it came to regulations and taking care of the vehicles, he was really strict."

Guys who worked with him say that Cashe did not cut corners. "Al used to sweat the details, and he was one of the most stubborn people I've met in my entire life," Ryan said. "He was tough and competitive, and he just wouldn't quit. He could be a pain in the ass if he thought you were getting something wrong, but you knew he cared about the mission, he cared about getting things done, and he cared about taking care of his people."

Ryan trusted Cashe's judgment. "One morning," Ryan said, "our commander asked me to go down and meet with the director of a school by the Tigris River about some things they needed. We rolled out in the Bradleys to the school compound. I went inside and was about to sit down with the schoolmaster when I got a call on the radio saying that our guys had just found a 122-millimeter mortar round in the ground, right in front of the school."

It turned out to be what's called a lollipop: a wire connected to a nine-volt battery. One of Ryan's squad leaders found the wire and traced it back to six bombs that had been daisy-chained together. Ryan had stepped right over it.

"Just Calm Down; It's Okay"

"Our guys called Explosive Ordnance Disposal [EOD] to come over to clear it out," Ryan recalled, "and I told the principal to gather the kids in this courtyard inside the school so that no one would get hurt when EOD blew the bomb up.

"We were waiting for a long time, and I started to get

paranoid, feeling stuck in the courtyard with the students and the staff. I started yelling questions into my radio, asking about everyone's status.

"Right away, I heard Cashe's voice over the radio, saying 'Just calm down; it's okay. I got everybody.'"

That was all Cashe needed to say.

"I trusted him completely, and it felt really good to have him come on the radio and tell me everything was fine," Ryan said. "If he told me everything was under control, I knew it was. Nobody got hurt, although when they detonated the bomb, it was powerful enough to blow out six windows in the front of the school."

Ryan said that he and Cashe usually stuck to the business at hand when they were out on patrol with each other, so he was surprised one day when Cashe looked sideways at Ryan as they were driving on a familiar route, near their base, and then stared ahead at the road as he said, "You know, the worst thing that's going to happen to us is going to happen right here."

Ryan disagreed, saying that they had always been careful not to set patterns and that this wasn't a road that they ever had to think too hard about.

Cashe shook his head. "That's why we're going to get hit hard here sometime," Cashe said. His words proved prophetic, because that was the road on which the Bradley was ambushed a few months later.

"I Wish That I Had Been There"

Most leaders have their platoons for six months to a year. Ryan had already been a platoon leader for nine months before they deployed. His commander wanted him to return to the United States to finish his college degree. Eventually, at the sixteen-month mark, Ryan agreed. He left Iraq in May 2005, five months before the ambush. "I have a lot of guilt about what happened after I left, not because I think I'm so special that I could have made things work out differently," he said. "But I wish that I had been there anyway, fighting alongside them."

No one could have predicted how any individual would have responded to the ambush, according to Ryan. "Some people have a parasympathetic response in a crisis; they freeze or drop the phone. Other people get an adrenaline rush and take action. You just don't know what you have in you, what you are capable of. Al exceeded every imaginable expectation of how you would expect a brother to respond that day."

I agree. Remember, Cashe was injured but not seriously wounded from the initial explosion. He entered a burning Bradley that was under enemy fire three times, while he himself was on fire, to ensure the safety of every member of his unit.

The story of Cashe's bravery moves me. I have run into fire. It's a hard thing to do even when you are wearing a mask and specialized fire-retardant gear. The heat hits you and singes your eyebrows. If you have ever leaned into a pizza oven, you have felt a tiny fraction of the kind of heat that Cashe confronted and chose to plunge into, over and over again.

I'm sure that Cashe's adrenaline was flowing, but he would have had to make a conscious decision to run into those flames three times. He is a hero and he deserves the Medal of

Honor. "No one wins this award; they earn it by their performance in situations no one would ever want to be in," Ryan said. "They demonstrate a willingness to die so that others can live."

TYRONE WOODS AND GLEN DOHERTY

One of the reasons that I want people to understand the truth about what happened in Benghazi is because Tyrone "Rone" Woods and Glen "Bub" Doherty gave their lives that night. All of the surviving members of our team want to make sure that their bravery and sacrifice are documented accurately, from the perspective of the men who were with them on the ground.

Everyone on our team was former special ops or Marines, but no one quibbled about gear or skills once all night. I think it's fair to say that we let Rone lead the way when we were going out and that he didn't think twice. He respected everyone on our team and he had earned everyone's respect. He wasn't trying to boss anyone around; he just had a natural authority and presence that made you trust him. Rone was a former SEAL Team 6, and he was a huge guy. I've described the feeling of going into battle with him as being like going into combat with Leonidas, the warrior king of Sparta. Rone died after holding a fighting position on top of Building C in the Annex for over eight hours.

Bub was a member of the Tripoli-based GRS team that had chartered a private airplane from an oil executive to get the team from Tripoli to Benghazi to help us. We joked about that plane later, teasing about those guys flying to us in style on a G6 with fancy leather seats. But the truth is that was the only air support we got, and that isn't a joke. We did not have any US air assets that night. I am not going to hash over in these pages why that happened or how that decision got made. I am not in a position to know for sure. What I do know is that if Bub and his team had not brought us that plane, Dave Ubben and Oz Geist might very well have died.

Bub was the only one of the Tripoli-based team to climb up onto Building C and connect with Rone, Oz, and Dave, who were still in their fighting positions after holding them all night.

I remember hearing a sound like a rocket being launched, like a swoosh. It did not have the distinct sound of a mortar being fired in its tube. The first explosion missed the back side of Building C, and then gunfire erupted behind it and a fresh wave of attacks began to assault the back side of our compound. One mortar after another hit, and explosive lights filled my night-vision goggles, blinding me with a wall of charged, sparkling dust. When it cleared, I could no longer see or hear any of my teammates on the top of Building C.

Rone and Bub died in that attack, and Dave and Oz were seriously wounded. By the time we evacuated everyone from the Annex and the mission to the airport at six in the morning, Bub's chartered airplane was still the only one there. There wasn't room for everyone on that plane, but Dave and Oz were flown to Tripoli for the medical attention that saved their lives. Those of us who stayed behind didn't see another airplane for more than four hours.

The truth is that all of our guys in Benghazi acted honorably. Everyone continually risked his own life to save other people. We went into a situation where we were under-manned and where we had given up the initiative to the enemy when we were forced to wait. Every one of us got into our vehicles knowing that we didn't have enough personnel and thinking that we didn't have as many weapons systems as the enemy did. Yet we drove right into the battle, determined not to leave anyone behind. That is personal courage and that is honor.

DAN LAGUNA

I appreciate how difficult it is to act with honor and to go above and beyond in an extreme situation. One of my earliest encounters with a VBIED took place in Baghdad in 2005, and I think about it a lot because I believe I came up short.

I was on the ground running security as the detail leader for a visit that the acting ambassador was making to the compound of a local imam. It was not a covert operation. We were the visible security for the Department of State during a long, hot day, and the visit attracted a lot of local attention. The atmosphere was tense.

When the meeting ended, I traveled ahead of the ambassador's detail with a military Humvee to set up a tactical control point (TCP) for his trip back to the embassy. That just means that I was setting up a kind of checkpoint or blocking position at an intersection so that the person I was protecting could speed through quickly and thereby avoid any possible attack.

We waited for approximately thirty minutes for the ambassador at that TCP, and traffic really backed up. This made me nervous because people were getting angry as the

minutes ticked by and the situation felt potentially volatile. Another US military convoy of Humvees heading in the
other direction was waiting to move, and after the ambassador finally came through, I guided the Humvees through to
bypass the line while we continued to hold the TCP for the
trail team that would be following the ambassador.

A few minutes later, the ground rocked from a huge explosion. A VBIED had detonated at the imam's compound. I
could see the mushroom cloud of smoke and debris rise from
my checkpoint, but we were about a hundred meters or so
away, so I didn't catch any shrapnel.

I called the trail team on the radio, confirmed that they
were okay, and held the checkpoint for them to come through.
Our whole team was intact, but as we raced back into the
Green Zone, I saw one of the helicopters peel back to the site
of the explosion.

The convoy that I had shepherded through the TCP had
gotten hit in the explosion. Dan Laguna, a former Green
Beret and a former pilot with the 160th Special Operations
Aviation Regiment, was flying back to the scene, and he
wound up collecting a soldier from the Humvee that had
been hit and flying him back for medical help.

I am ashamed to say that I was so focused on getting my
team out and completing the mission that I didn't think to
peel off and go back to help until much later.

"I Had to Get Back"

Dan exemplifies honor to me because he went back to try
to save lives. Dan had been through multiple deployments,
including Iraq, Bosnia, and Somalia, so it doesn't surprise me
that he was the first one to turn around toward the fire to save

lives. I talked to him afterward and asked him about his decision. He just said, "Our people were injured. I had to get back."

His words hit me hard. I knew that I had not done anything wrong, but I regretted not having taken that next step once I had confirmed the security of my own team. I should have gone back right away to see if anyone needed my help. I don't know if Dan knew to do this because he had made a mistake once upon a time or because he is just a deeply honorable man. He saved a life. His example has stayed with me, and it may have played a role in strengthening my resolve during Benghazi.

LEARN FROM MISTAKES

In Benghazi, on September 11, 2012, there was a moment when the back gate to the compound was open and I had two choices: I could find good cover, which might have given the enemy time to get through that gate, or I could take a knee out in the open and shoot through the back gate to keep the enemy from advancing through it, like the Rangers who served in Operation Just Cause during the invasion of Panama in 1989. Those Rangers landed on Rio Hato Airfield without any cover and stood their ground and shot at the enemy until they were able to advance off the tarmac. I thought about those guys at that moment in Benghazi when I decided that my best cover might be to shoot on the offensive.

I took a knee, made myself as small as I possibly could, and fired through that gate so that nobody else got through. Dave "Boone" Benton still gives me a hard time about that decision; he says that it was a stupid risk. I stand by it. Five or ten seconds is all the time a bunch of bad guys needed to run through the gate. If I can shoot like hell and use bullets as my cover while my partner takes cover and gets a better fighting position, maybe it helps us down the road.

Yes, it was a risky move, but not a stupid one. It was my conscious decision to take a knee. I had a split second to choose. My thought processes were not exactly instinctive. During my years of training and deployments, I had war-gamed different experiences. I knew from my training, and from my experience shooting at night, that because the snapping sound of the rounds was high, it meant that the bullets were going over my head. I was guessing that the enemy didn't have night-vision goggles and couldn't adjust their sights, which might keep me safer. I had trained for that decision.

Starved and Sleep-Deprived

Upon graduation from Ranger School in December 2000, I got a few weeks' leave and went to see my family. They were shocked by my appearance. Remember, I had just finished Ranger School, so I had been starved and sleep-deprived and made to run seven-minute miles with a fifty-pound ruck on my back as part of my training. I was run-down and almost emaciated. I got some rest and recovered some during my leave, but I was still skinny when I reported for duty.

At Fort Knox, Kentucky, we did a complex training op with the 160th Special Operations Aviation Regiment, some pararescuemen, combat controllers, and Air Force special operations pilots.

An elaborate model city had been constructed for units to conduct different Military Operations in Urban Terrain

(MOUT) training missions. We would be doing fast-rope insertions from MH-53 Pave Low helicopters.

Black Hawks are easier to get out of, but I think fast roping is more fun than jumping, so I was looking forward to being in the Pave Lows. Pave Low helicopters have large blades that create a powerful rotary wash. Normally, a rope hangs down from a helicopter more or less like a pole, but in a Pave Low, it doesn't matter how high up you are, the rope comes off the back of the bird at a forty-five-degree angle. Imagine sliding down a fire pole at that angle in midair.

It's extremely difficult to hold on with your feet, so you are sliding down at an angle with just your hands.

It was raining as we came flying in on the Pave Lows. From the drop, my team did a five-mile hump, up a muddy hill, wearing fifty-pound rucks. We had to be in position at a particular time to provide suppressive fire. I was a machine gunner, so I was carrying that extra weight as well, but even so, it was taking me more effort to keep up with everybody than normal.

It turned out that I was developing ulcerative colitis, but I didn't know that. Instead, I thought I might have still been rebuilding my strength after having had it torn down during Ranger School. It was February in Kentucky, so it was cold and the leaves on the ground had turned into mush. Halfway up the hill, I was smoked. One of the other gunners took my gun and carried it up the hill for me. It was humbling, but he got my gun up there, along with his, in time for both of us to be in position and fulfill our mission.

To an unschooled listener, the scene might have sounded like nothing but chaos, but there was a rhythm and coordination among the weapons. Our guns were rattling as we put rounds on our targets, but it was like a symphony, with each gun taking a break in turn so that the barrels could cool and we could avoid a cook-off while continuing to fire. I could hear the guns talking to each other. It sounded like we knew what the hell we were doing.

"You Just Got Shot"

We had OCs, or observer-controllers, leaders who were essentially grading our activity in the mission. Our OC, Captain Harmon, was the commanding company officer of the 2nd Battalion 75th HQ company element. At some point during the mission, I was trying to take cover behind a bus, but part of my leg was sticking out. Harmon saw me and hit me hard in the leg. "You just got shot," he said.

He was right. I needed to be completely covered. I had a lot of cover around me and it was lazy not to pull my leg in. I paid the price. My buddy put a tourniquet on me, as though I had been wounded, and I had to lie there until the op was over.

EMBRACING THE VALUES
HONOR

Honor incorporates all of the values you should have in every aspect of your life. Living honorably means that you do the right thing, even when no one is watching. Especially when no one is watching, and even when you know that you will not be judged, rewarded, or reprimanded. It is easier to display honorable behavior when we are being watched.

Honorable behavior is often assessed after a battle between you and your conscience, and that can make it difficult to commit to sometimes. Don't bullshit yourself.

It is honorable to take a job that requires you to be willing to give your life for anyone who needs it. If your job is to respond to an accident, to fight a fire, to stop traffic, to put yourself in the middle of a fight, or to walk into a house or a situation that everyone else is running out of, you are doing honorable work.

The military and paramilitary organizations demand honorable behavior from their members at home, too.

But honorable behavior is important in the civilian world, too. You can hold yourself to the same standard, no matter what you do for a living, or what circumstances you find yourself in.

Acting honorably doesn't mean you don't screw up. Honorable people make mistakes. There will be mission failures, bad decisions, even bad shoots. No one is perfect. You need to have the guts to speak up, to call things out, to note the violations, the dangers, and situations where standards are not being upheld. In Benghazi, we had people in charge of security who were not knowledgeable about security. It cost people's lives. You can read about those errors and their consequences in the book *13 Hours: The Inside Account of What Really Happened in Benghazi*, which I cowrote with my surviving teammates and Mitchell Zuckoff.

If you are the problem, all is not lost. You can still be honorable: just own your problem and fix it. I have not always acted with integrity, and I have learned from my failures. I think most of us know when we are lacking in integrity. I know, deep in my gut, when I have made decisions that were wrong. Sometimes I have corrected course; sometimes I have tried to rationalize the decision; and sometimes I went ahead anyway, knowing that I was being selfish. I am human and I am weak. I know that I need to accept responsibility for my mistakes, and I know that they will haunt me until I repair and repent.

Don't take the easy way out. Commit to being honorable, even if doing so is sometimes painful. If someone needs help, run toward them and help. Know that, in the long run, you will be more at peace.

CHAPTER EIGHT

INTEGRITY

Do what's right, legally and morally. Integrity is a quality you develop by adhering to moral principles. It requires that you do and say nothing that deceives others. As your integrity grows, so does the trust others place in you. The more choices you make based on integrity, the more this highly prized value will affect your relationships with family and friends, and, finally, the fundamental acceptance of yourself.

DOING THE RIGHT THING WHEN NO one else is looking is not always easy. We can't always be watched and we shouldn't need watching. People of integrity tell the truth. Sometimes integrity feels like the most difficult of all the values to practice consistently, but I know I need to get it right if I want to be a trustworthy person. Integrity is at the core of every functional relationship, both at work and at home.

In a combat situation, everyone in the unit needs to be reliable. We may need to run toward fire together, take a bunker out, or rescue one another. Anything could happen. If I don't feel like the person standing next to me is going to have my back, my performance will suffer. If I hear that someone is stealing gear, or having an affair, or cutting corners, or just not meeting standards, I may feel that I cannot trust that person. If someone is engaging in those behaviors, it suggests that he thinks, "I am more important than other people. My happiness, my pleasure, my interests, are more important than those of other people, including members of my team."

That attitude does not inspire confidence, and the resulting mistrust can have life-or-death consequences. I need to trust that the person next to me in combat will have total integrity and that he will lay down his life for me if he has to, just as I would for him.

It is important that we hold ourselves to a high standard, even if the stakes do not always seem so high in the civilian world. I want to be a person of integrity because I want to be a good person and a good citizen, not just because I'm an instructor, or because I am working as an operator downrange and I want everyone to come home safely. I want to hold myself to the higher standard because it is the right thing to do. Everyone needs to figure out why integrity matters for themselves.

There have been moments in my life that I am not proud of, moments when I have displayed a lack of integrity. I have also been betrayed by other people who lacked integrity. Most people have probably been in both positions. That is okay; that is how some people learn.

But I have never been in either situation in the 75th Ranger Regiment, not even once. I believe that one of the reasons that our team in Benghazi ran toward that fire and was able to function so effectively through the night was that we were all former Marines or special operations guys that had integrity toward each other.

A New Path

I miss deploying, but I believe that God has put me on a new path for a purpose. I have come to believe that one of those reasons has been for me to learn from the examples, strength, and integrity of other soldiers and their families. It is my privilege to shine a light on the stories of other men and women who have served with honor.

When troops are deployed overseas for a long time, many people at home begin to pay less attention to our casualties and the consequences of our battles. The US military has been fighting in the Middle East for a long time now. The United States has been at war in Afghanistan since 2001. Operation Iraqi Freedom lasted from 2003 to 2011 and was preceded by troops on the ground there in 1990 and 1991 for the Persian Gulf War.

We need to pay attention not only to the extraordinary sacrifices that have been made on the battlefield, but also to the ordinary, specific lives that have been lost for our country. I don't care where you fall on the political spectrum; I believe it our patriotic duty to honor the memory and the sacrifice of our soldiers and their families.

RYAN DOLTZ

A company called Fox Trail Productions has created a pro-military documentary series called *War Heroes*, which profiles the real-life stories of American soldiers. I was proud to host the pilot episode, which focuses on the life and death of Sergeant Ryan Doltz of the New Jersey National Guard.

I spent time with Ryan's family, friends, and some of the guys he served with, to learn about him. Our team didn't just want to know about what Ryan did; we also wanted to know who he was.

Ryan Doltz was born in 1978 and grew up in Morris County, New Jersey. According to his family, he always loved the military, even as a young boy. Ryan was an energetic, athletic guy. He earned a black belt in karate, played football and baseball at Dover High School, and was happiest when he was working to get stronger.

Ryan entered the Virginia Military Institute directly out of high school, as a member of the class of 2000. Ryan's mother, Cheryl, told me that Ryan seemed to embrace the structure of military life and was proud to be a part of the VMI tradition.

VMI is a tough place. Freshmen are called rats, and they are put on the so-called rat line, where they are physically challenged and taught how to march and how to study, an intense process that is meant to serve up some pain with a purpose.

Before they are trained to become leaders, cadets are taught to serve and follow. Ryan worked hard to succeed academically, and he thrived as a member of the VMI community. Ryan was a big guy: six feet six and 250 pounds. He entered VMI as a football player, but an injury led him to switch to rugby ("football without pads," as he called it). Ryan also played tuba in the Band Company. Cheryl jokes that "the tuba was perfect for Ryan because he was big enough to handle it."

One of the stories that people at VMI still love to tell about Ryan is how he helped with a raid, led by his friends Howie Cook and Mike Judge, to steal a Jeep that belonged to the commandant at the Citadel, VMI's great football rival. The Jeep was presented to the Citadel officer at the annual game.

"Babyface" Ryan

Ryan also gained some attention when he was one of four VMI cadets chosen to participate in a television commercial for Norelco razors that was filmed on the VMI campus. His star appearance resulted in his getting the nickname "Baby-face," which he accepted with his usual good nature.

In 1998, while he was still at VMI, Ryan joined the Virginia Army National Guard. He won a Top Gun Award for military proficiency at section tasks associated with 13B10 training and earned his emergency medical technician certification in Virginia. As a member of A Battery 1/246th Field Artillery in Martinsville, Virginia, Ryan was activated shortly after his graduation in 2002 as part of Operation Noble Eagle (ONE).

ONE began in response to the attacks of September 11, 2001. This US and Canadian military operation related to homeland security provided support to federal, state, and local agencies, and it continues today. Ryan spent a year on active duty at Aberdeen Proving Ground in Maryland.

In 2003, Ryan moved home and transferred to the 3/112th Field Artillery of the New Jersey National Guard, based in Morristown, New Jersey. He also began working as a cost engineer for Moretrench American Corporation, an engineering firm that was rebuilding a wall that had been part of the World Trade Center towers. Ryan became certified as an EMT in New Jersey and volunteered for the Mine Hill First Aid Squad, along with his younger brother, Gregory. Ryan was back with his family, serving his community, and figuring out his life's path.

In January 2004, Ryan's National Guard unit was activated to take part in Operation Iraqi Freedom.

Ryan's unit was sent to Fort Dix, New Jersey, to train for deployment to perform military police duties. During the training, Ryan fractured both heels and was sent home with an initial prognosis that he might be in a wheelchair for six weeks and then need physical therapy for six months before he would be able to deploy.

But Ryan wanted to go to Iraq with the guys whom he knew and trusted, so he worked hard to prove the doctors wrong.

After several months of determined physical work, Ryan convinced the doctors that he had healed enough to be deployed; he landed in Iraq on April 9, 2004.

"He could have been excused through the summer," Ryan's mother told me, "but he wanted to be with his unit."

Ryan's unit was stationed outside Sadr City, a Baghdad suburb that was one of the country's most volatile regions. They were Charlie company, Jersey guys, 180 mostly artillery men whose main mission was to patrol the area, to safeguard Iraqi police stations, and to provide security and drivers to various military convoys.

"This Is Where We Should Be"

Ryan kept in touch with his family while he was in Iraq, usually calling home once a week when he was back at his base, according to Cheryl. "He was optimistic," she said, "and he told me, 'This is where we should be' and hoped he was making a difference. He was all about his men and the mission."

On June 5, 2004, the vehicle that Ryan was driving hit an IED as he was providing security for a convoy returning to their base. Ryan was killed immediately, along with Staff Sergeant Humberto Timoteo. Ryan was the third soldier from New Jersey to die during the global war on terror.

Ryan was posthumously promoted to the rank of sergeant and awarded the Bronze Star, the Purple Heart, and the Good Conduct Medal. He was laid to rest in Arlington National

Cemetery. The funeral in New Jersey attracted throngs, and more than three hundred people attended the burial itself, a testament to the impact he had had on others and to the kind of man he was, according to Cheryl.

"Ryan was not an officer, just an average person," she said. "Ryan Edward Doltz was an American patriot in the truest sense of the word. He was willing to put his own hopes and dreams on hold because he felt that his country needed him. He was a true citizen-soldier."

The Doltz family, like all Gold Star families, has sacrificed and suffered for our country. The public response to Ryan's death is a reflection of Ryan's character and of his family's contributions to their community. Ryan's father is a former chief of the Mine Hill Fire Department and his mother is an elementary school teacher. More than one hundred residents of Mine Hill who attended Ryan's funeral then traveled the 250 miles to Arlington to attend his burial.

I have lost friends in combat, and I think about them every day. I can't imagine what it would be like to lose a family member in combat. I admire the way that the Doltz family has worked to preserve Ryan's story and memory and turn his death into an opportunity for positive change. They have created a foundation called the SGT Ryan E. Doltz Memorial Foundation. Ryan's sister, Anne, is the head of the nonprofit foundation, which has established scholarships to support the education of college-bound students from Morris County, New Jersey, for members or dependents of members of the New Jersey National Guard, and for VMI cadets.

The foundation has established investment accounts to support two young sons of other fallen soldiers in Ryan's unit, and the foundation contributes to other organizations and efforts to support military families in need. The Doltz family has continued to share Ryan's story, which I know can be difficult, because they are committed to honoring his sacrifice.

Members of the Doltz family have demonstrated patience and dignity through their loss. On the day that Ryan died, a young photographer from *Newsweek* magazine took pictures of the scene of the aftermath of the attack that killed Ryan. The photographer took pictures of soldiers removing Ryan's body from his Humvee, and *Newsweek* published one of them.

The Doltz family had no idea the photographs existed and did not receive any warning about the publication. The first time that the Doltz family saw these pictures was in the pages of the magazine. That is horseshit. When Cheryl told me about the pictures, I felt my blood starting to boil just thinking about how she must have felt. Yet the Doltz family handled this outrageous situation with so much strength. Cheryl Doltz called *Newsweek* and explained, like the teacher she is, how those photographs made her feel. Cheryl ultimately met with the photographer and told me that the photographer was devastated to see the effect of his photographs on her family. I imagine and hope that he and his editors learned something.

Cheryl Doltz's ability to forgive and to make something constructive out of a bad situation humbles me. I understand what it feels like to have my story be manipulated or used for someone else's purposes. The Doltz family has more reason to be pissed off at the media than I have ever had, and they have been forgiving. It was instructive for me to spend time with them and study the example of their conduct.

Cheryl Doltz honors her son's memory by embracing others instead of hating the world. It would be tempting to turn inward and give up after suffering the kind of loss that the Doltz family has endured. Instead, they have derived meaning from their loss. Their integrity is inspiring and healing for me to witness. The Doltz family is living a heroic life.

EMBRACING THE VALUES
INTEGRITY

I am a Christian. In my faith, the Ten Commandments tell me how to behave, and they line up with the Army Values. I know that I have said that we have to do the right thing when no one is watching, but I also believe that God is always watching and that He offers opportunities and lessons.

Whether I choose to learn a lesson or repeat a mistake is up to me. It is up to me to become a person with more integrity and to figure out what helps me to live up to the best version of myself.

My work, faith, and values help me to have integrity. I think I have been at my best when I was deploying. My vow to be a good operator was paramount, and it kept me focused on my job.

Selfishness is often at the core of a lack of integrity. In combat situations, if someone lacks integrity, they may not put themselves out in front. You can't put yourself first in the military; most of the time your job requires you to prioritize the needs of others. It often takes more effort to do that at home, or in a civilian job, where the consequences of putting yourself first may not be so dire.

The people in your life should know that they can count on you. If members of a unit don't feel that everyone is reliable, that unit will be weak. That applies outside the military, too. It is true of a family, an organization, or a working group. If the guy next to me demonstrates a lack of integrity, even about something that may seem to have nothing to do with me directly, it will still affect me. A group member's poor behavior suggests that they think, "I am the most important thing. You aren't. My pleasure, my happiness, my self are more important than you guys. I just want to be happy or feel good, and it doesn't matter how it makes you feel."

That way of thinking makes me think that I can't trust you, and it will affect our interactions. In a unit, you need to have complete confidence and trust in the person next to you. If you want them to feel the same way about you, you have to be a person of integrity.

CHAPTER NINE

PERSONAL COURAGE

Face fear, danger or adversity (physical or moral). Personal courage has long been associated with our Army. With physical courage, it is a matter of enduring physical duress and at times risking personal safety. Facing moral fear or adversity may be a long, slow process of continuing forward on the right path, especially if taking those actions is not popular with others. You can build your personal courage by daily standing up for and acting upon the things that you know are honorable.

SOMETIMES I THINK THAT PHYSICAL COURAGE, the kind you need in order to run toward gunfire or into a burning building, is easier to summon than moral courage. That has been true for me. Research suggests that when we are faced with a significant physical risk we will go into a kind of robot mode and fall back on our highest level of training.

I have found this to be true. The first time I jumped out of an airplane, I was going to be the first person out, so I got to stand at the door when it opened. I felt the force of the air as it came blasting into the fuselage. I looked down and watched the tops of the trees rush by in a blur as I waited for that green light to tell me to jump. Every nerve in my body was telling me that nothing was normal and that I should not jump out of the plane. I tried to calm myself by reviewing all the steps I would need to follow, but I was still nervous.

Yet when the green light turned on, that was it, and I threw myself out the door. That is a form of physical courage, and I have always been pretty good at that.

Moral courage can be more challenging. It is scary to confront obstacles. It is brave to make changes in your life. It can take courage to refuse to do something you know is wrong, even more so when other people around you are doing it.

It can be hard to put other people's interests and feelings before your own. But I can feel myself get stronger, both morally and mentally, when I make the right choices, and that leads me to be happier and more at peace. If you know how to use it, fear can be a kind of fuel to help you make hard choices correctly and stick to the right path.

When I joined the Army, I knew I would be facing physical and mental challenges, but I was also facing an overriding fear of the unknown. I was starting something new and wondering what I was getting myself into. Sometimes I worried about whether I was going to be able to handle the obstacles that the Army would purposefully place in front of me, but my fears extended beyond failing to meet standards. Joining the military meant that I was giving up a large measure of control over my life.

In the civilian world, and even many paramilitary jobs, your time is your own when you are off the clock. In the military, I was never really off the clock. I was subject to civilian law, military law, the rules of my unit, and, in my case, *The Ranger Blue Book*.

A Higher Standard

The rules for soldiers extend to aspects of our lives that are less likely to be regulated in the real world. If I were to violate the rules of the *Ranger Blue Book*, which is specific to the 75th

Ranger Regiment, I could be RFS (relief for standards). In plain English, I could get kicked out of Ranger Battalion. The rules covered behaviors such as drinking and driving, drug use, and when we could—and could not—leave the base.

The Ranger compound was isolated inside a chain-link fence with mesh woven through the links and concertina wire on portions of the top. No one could see inside. Whenever we left the compound, we were potentially visible to the public, and the Blue Book was specific about how we needed to appear: if we were not wearing civvies (civilian clothes), we had better be in starch and spits and a beret. That meant that my uniform needed to be starched, my boots needed to be spit shined, and my beret needed to be on the top of my head. Leaving the base wearing a training uniform, or what we called a fluff-and-buff uniform (something just out of the dryer) would have been grounds for an RFS.

To be a Ranger, I gave up some privacy and certain freedoms. I was volunteering to hold myself to a higher standard. That is one reason I reflexively respect veterans and servicemen and women: their military status tells me that they have chosen to be held to a higher standard. Many paramilitary organizations, like police departments and fire departments, also require their members to be subject to exacting standards. The question, for any organization, is whether members are living up to the standards and how seriously the standards are enforced. The Rangers were deadly serious about enforcing their standards. I saw guys kicked out for drinking, drug use, for fighting on the weekends, and for similar infractions.

Trusting that your teammates are meeting standards is essential. When our squad set out on a mission in Ranger Battalion, one person had to be in charge. I might not have made the same decision my leader made each time, but I trusted my squad leaders and understood that our perspectives were different. The leader needs to anticipate every possible scenario, positive or negative, visualize the outcome, determine the course of action, and communicate it clearly. He or she may have information as a leader that I don't have. I need to trust that the leader knows what to do, and he or she needs to rely on me to do exactly what I have been ordered to do.

Our team that worked so well together in Benghazi may have been made up of guys from different branches of the armed forces, but we all had committed to meeting high standards. We were all experienced operators, we had all survived demanding training, and we were all willing to sacrifice our lives for others. We may have had disagreements, but everyone was able to set them aside or resolve them so that they did not interfere with our mission. The trust that we had in each other helped us to be courageous.

It is easier to have courage when you have support. When I trust that everyone around me is operating effectively, I find it easier to do my job. I don't think about death. I don't think about losing. I think, "I am going to go in there and kick the shit out of this mission. I don't care if the odds are one hundred to one against us."

That is the mentality that I need to have when I am summoning up physical courage, and I think that attitude is contagious. Courage breeds courage just as panic breeds panic. When we were fighting in Benghazi, I had a feeling of courage that spread like a fire, and moments where I felt like I was ten feet tall and could take on the world. I attribute that confidence to our team: no one expressed a moment of doubt, and our courage fed each other.

EVERYDAY COURAGE

On some level, I don't know what was so special about our behavior in Benghazi. I truly believe that anyone who found themselves in my situation, who had served and was trained to fight, would have stepped up and done the same thing, especially if they were part of the same kind of kick-ass team. I appreciate that people are interested in understanding that battle, and I have come to think that part of the interest is because everyone is fighting a battle of their own.

For example, it can take genuine courage to confront a health issue. I love it when someone tells me that something in my story helped them want to become stronger or more physically fit. I am something of an evangelical runner, so I get a kick out of the readers who start running, even though that isn't something that I write much about.

I'm thinking about a guy who started running and stopped drinking, someone else who is training for her first half marathon, and a woman who started running and lost fifty pounds. It makes my day when people let me know that there was something in my book or one of my speeches that helped them summon the courage to confront a problem and over-come adversity in their lives.

Every one of the warriors you have read about in this book has displayed an impressive measure of personal courage beyond the battlefield. They may have witnessed violence and tragedy, sustained life-altering injuries, and confronted unexpected obstacles in their life paths. It would have been easy for most of them to descend into a permanent state of anger or disappointment. It is challenging to live life with a sense of optimism and purpose after experiencing the tragedy of watching your friends die. It can require an enormous amount of moral and physical courage just to live a heroic life.

TOM BLOCK

Sergeant Tom Block is a retired Ranger from the 3rd Battalion, 75th Ranger Regiment, who deployed four times in support of Operation Enduring Freedom, which ran from 2001 to 2014, primarily in Afghanistan.

In some ways, Tom's identity has been defined by his physical strength and courage. "I grew up fighting," Tom said. "I was the runt of the litter and used to getting knocked around by my older cousins. I had to get tough fast, and I loved it. It translated well to wrestling."

Tom wrestled at Waseca High School in Minnesota and Minnesota State University, Mankato. He enlisted in the Army in February of 2010, and he distinguished himself right away. Tom was an honor grad, combatives champ (hand-to-hand fighting), and four points away from being the PT stud for his Ranger Assessment and Selection Program class, almost pulling off a hat trick.

"I love a good scrap, even if I lose," Tom said. "When we were doing combative training, I was always the guy volunteering to get in the big fight suit."

Tom also volunteered to wear the bite suit when his unit worked with K-9 dogs and their trainers. "That is a unique experience, to have ninety pounds of fury coming down on you and to try to protect yourself and fight them back," he said. Tom is as tough as they come.

Tom was on his fourth combat rotation when he was

severely wounded in October 2013, when a bomber detonated herself near his assault force in Kandahar Province, Afghanistan. Tom was hurled thirty-five feet into a minefield. Four people died on that mission, and two dozen were wounded.

Tom has been awarded the Purple Heart, the Joint Service Commendation Medal, the Army Commendation Medal, the Army Achievement Medal, the Army Good Conduct Medal, the National Defense Service Medal, the Afghanistan Campaign Medal with Combat Star, the Global War on Terrorism Service Medal, the Army Service Ribbon, the Overseas Service Ribbon, and the NATO Medal. In 2014, the *Army Times* named Tom as its Soldier of the Year.

But the price was steep. Tom sustained a collapsed lung, significant leg injuries, a broken foot, and multiple shrapnel and burn wounds in the attack. The entire right side of Tom's face was smashed, and he lost most of his nose, his right eye, and most of his vision in his left eye.

He replaced his right eye with a prosthetic eye that bears the Captain America shield, which he described as a symbol of hope as well as a symbol that his life had changed.

"I opted out of having a prosthetic eye painted to match my real eye," he said. "I didn't want to pretend to have a normal eye, to pretend to be the same. I know I'm not the same man I was before the incident. To me, the Captain America eye represents that change."

"I Wanted Revenge"

Some people don't acknowledge the eye when they meet Tom, a failure that bothers him. "Maybe they aren't sure if they should say something, but I want people to acknowledge it," he said. "Someone who buys a Corvette doesn't do it to be inconspicuous. I wanted this eye to be something special, to inspire and motivate others to not let life beat them down. Maybe this eye is just my way to raise a middle finger to terrorists."

In November 2013, about six weeks after the explosion, Tom was discharged from Walter Reed Hospital and relocated to the Minneapolis Polytrauma Rehabilitation Center, part of the VA system, to be closer to his family.

He was still in a wheelchair, but newly engaged. Tom, who had been dating Janine since 2012, was in intensive care, hooked up to machines, his face bandaged, and with tubes hanging everywhere, when he asked Janine's father for permission to marry her.

He said, "Steve, can I marry your daughter? I promise to take better care of her than I do myself."

After being discharged from the Minneapolis VA, Tom visited Fort Benning, Georgia, and met his platoon when they returned from deployment on December 7, 2013. The last time these men had seen Tom was in the hospital in Kandahar, when doctors were unsure of his prognosis. Four members of the platoon had died and twenty-four had been injured, including Tom. "That was a big day," he said. "I was able to stand up and get out of my wheelchair to greet them. It was emotional for all of us."

Tom's recovery and rehabilitation were just beginning. He relearned how to walk, and he still can't run on his right leg as well as he used to before the explosion. As his mobility improved, he was assigned to be a noncommissioned officer in charge of the gym in Alabama.

He was not going to be able to return to the work he had done before, but the assignment allowed him to continue to improve his strength and conditioning as he helped others train. Matt Powell, the strength and conditioning coach of the 3rd Battalion, encouraged Tom to work out harder. "It was tough," Tom said. "Matt pushed me when I didn't want to be pushed. He pushed me when I would start to feel sorry for myself."

In all, Tom has undergone fifteen surgeries to rebuild his face. But his face was not the only thing that needed help during the first years after the attack. His soul did, too.

"I was so angry," he said. "I wanted revenge. I still feel like I never got to hit back or exact revenge the way I would have wanted to, but I don't think about that as much as I used to."

Tom's wounds forced him to medically retire from the Army in February of 2016. He remained upbeat, but it was a tough transition: "Growing up, I was a physical-minded person. This was different for me. It wasn't something I could just punch through or lift out of the way."

But Tom had absorbed the "never quit" ethos of the Ranger Regiment. "I don't give up," he said. "My story got a lot of attention and I feel like I have to move forward to set a good example for others to follow."

And Tom also feels a responsibility as a Ranger: "If I identify myself as a Ranger, I have an obligation to maintain standards and I can't be a jerk."

During his years as a Ranger, Tom identified powerfully with his work. "Being a Ranger wasn't a sacrifice for me at all," he said. "I legit loved that job. It was my dream job. Every day was different. One day I might have been sitting in a Black Hawk, cruising down the Chattahoochee, and the next week I'm cleaning the barracks, so that the next week I can go jump out of airplanes again."

Tom had signed up for the military right from college: "I was a kid, and the Army trained me, gave me the clothes on my back, a bed to sleep in, a machine gun, and all the ammo I could hope for," he said.

Tom was young, gaining real-life experiences. "It was a great fit for me," he said of his training. "I have always been high energy. As a kid, I always pushed limits, even just grinding wheelies down a gravel driveway with complete disregard for my personal safety, hitting jumps and ramps and seeing how far I could get."

Tom began deploying in January 2011. All four of his tours were in Afghanistan, and they were busy deployments.

Adrenaline and Excitement and Fear

He loved that work, too. "I especially liked working at night; we owned the night," he said. Every Wednesday, Tom's unit would get an analysis of recent activity, which they would use to help plan their missions. "There were these color-coded bubbles that represented different areas and types of activity," he recalled. "When that map popped up and looked like a bag of Skittles on the ground, I would feel this great mix of adrenaline and excitement and fear."

When Tom was out on patrol, "there was no time to think about what if," he said. "I just accepted that whatever happened was going to happen, relied on my training, took my opportunities, and performed."

Defending the United States was a big part of what Tom liked about serving overseas. "When you travel to certain countries, you see the conditions and effects of true oppression. People living in those places do not know real freedom like Americans know it. Sometimes when I see what is taken for granted here in the United States, it chaps my ass a little bit. But that's part of what I fought for, right? For people to be blissfully ignorant back here in the bubble."

That can be difficult for people in the United States to relate to, especially those who have not traveled overseas to some of the places where Tom and I have worked.

"We do not struggle here in the same way," Tom said. "We are not a perfect country and we can improve, but people need to look around and realize how well we have it. My sense of patriotism grew after my first deployment. I saw how it could be in this world, with no infrastructure, no streetlights, no paved roads, filthy water, people crammed next to one another sleeping on floor mats, disease, poverty. It's not that many Americans don't struggle, but it really is on another level."

Many Americans also take some nonphysical aspects of our security for granted, Tom said. "In this country, you really can start with nothing and become successful, if you are willing to put the work in," he said. "And we have the right to disagree with the government and one another. There are a lot of people I do not agree with at all, but we share the freedom to speak up and conduct ourselves in whatever manner we decide to as long as we don't hurt each other. That is freedom, and that is worth dying for."

Tom's injuries made it impossible for him to continue working as a Ranger, so he looked around to find what he was going to do next and came across what seemed like the ideal next step. It was called the Human Exploitation Rescue Operative (HERO) Child-Rescue Corps, a partnership among the military, US Immigration and Customs Enforcement, and the National Association to Protect Children.

HERO Corps gives injured servicemen the opportunity to train in law enforcement, to learn specialized investigation skills and digital forensics, and to work to combat online child sexual exploitation by identifying and rescuing child victims.

Tom and his wife decided to move to Massachusetts so that Tom could work out of the Homeland Security Investigations field office in Boston. Tom's wife moved in January of 2016 and Tom was planning to join her in April, after completing his training for HERO Corps in Florida and Virginia.

But four months before he retired from the Army, Tom felt himself sliding into a depression. "My wife and I both had good jobs lined up, but I didn't really want to move," he said. "And my retirement from the military was about to be official, even though I was going to be working for HERO Corps."

"I Was Overwhelmed"

Tom had been a Ranger for most of his adult life. Now he found himself preparing to leave the Ranger Battalion, continuing to adjust to the physical and emotional damage he had sustained in the explosion, confronting his survivor's guilt, and entering into a marriage.

"All the urgent physical issues were being settled, but I was overwhelmed, and I really started to shut down," he said. "I started to drink too much."

Tom began to withdraw from his wife and to question their plans to move forward. "We were living separately because of my HERO Corps training, and I was calling her less and less," he said. "She gave me space, but she didn't want to quit. She was persistent, and, eventually, she challenged me to man up. I realized that our marriage and my new life might be a sinking ship, but that if I was going to go down, I wanted to go down guns blazing, knowing we had tried really hard to make everything work.

"I didn't know if it would work out, but I couldn't just quit."

Investigating Child Predators

In April 2016, Tom graduated from the HERO Corps program with sixteen other wounded, ill, or injured veterans and moved to Massachusetts, where he went to work.

Investigating child predators proved to be demanding and disturbing work, but Tom felt it was a worthwhile opportunity. "I thought it would be a great way to extend the mission I had in special operations," he said. "It was a mission to go after bad guys. I liked doing that and I wanted to continue doing that, even if I had to do it in a different way."

Tom's wife, Janine, turned out to be right. Their relationship improved. "We got better. I got better," Tom said. "I became more honest and more patient, with myself and with my wife. I had to work on accepting that nobody gets it right every time. It's okay to be wrong or make a mistake, as long as you are willing to correct it. That was a big thing for me to admit."

Tom didn't want to have any regrets, so he gave it his all. As we learned in Ranger School, you have to let your actions define your character, and you only know what is possible if you don't quit.

"If I quit on my recovery, I would feel like the terrorists won and I [had] become another casualty," Tom said. "My anger fueled my will to survive and to recover. I owe some of my willingness to push forward to a sense of defiance: if I give up or give in, the terrorists win."

Tom knows that anger can be effectively channeled as a positive force. "It's easy for guys like me to get angry and bitter, but you can use that anger toward a positive end," he said. "If you don't like something, be proactive and fix it or change it. Run for public office. Educate yourself. Tell your story. Help someone. Let your anger be an engine of change; don't get stuck in it."

Tom credits his recovery to the support he received from his wife, a small group of buddies from the military, and to the relief he feels when working out, particularly when training for Strongman competitions. Strongman competitions, which test the strength and endurance of athletes through weight-related events, like squats, deadlifts, and overhead presses, have become an important part of Tom's life.

"After I got blown up, I was sitting around for three years off and on between surgeries," he told me. "I did work out, but I didn't have a great focus, especially once I got through the initial injuries. I wasn't training to go overseas, so I didn't have to be fast, and I didn't need to work on skills like endurance for a particular mission. I needed a reason to train, and I guess not getting sloppy was not a strong enough reason."

Tom's trainer at 3rd Battalion, Matt Powell, suggested that Tom might enjoy setting a goal of competing in a Strongman event. When Tom moved to Boston, he joined a gym, Total Performance Sports, that focuses on power lifting, has Strongman equipment, and has hosted Strongman events.

Training for a contest and setting goals for each event gave Tom a sense of focus, and he turned out to be good at it, winning second place in the novice class for his first Strongman event in Boston.

"My Ultimate Competition Is Myself"

Tom continues to train to be at a competitive level of fitness and hopes that he will eventually earn his pro card, but he isn't motivated by lifting more than other people. Tom's overarching competitor is not the person he faces in any given event. "My biggest opponent is that voice inside me that says, 'This hurts and you can't do it,'" Tom said. "So my ultimate competition is myself, telling that little voice to shut the heck up."

The training has been positive for Tom's overall health. "Working out makes me stretch muscles and give my joints attention that I might not otherwise," he said. "If I didn't work out, I think I would be in more pain from my injuries."

The benefits have been more than physical ones. Tom has found a supportive community. "I have friends that I only know through Strongman," he said, "and it's good for me to meet like-minded people and lift heavy-ass stuff."

There was no magic moment when Tom came to terms with not working as a Ranger. Instead, he progressed steadily toward accepting his new reality. "I had to learn how to let things be," Tom said. "I can sit here and romanticize the way things used to be, but I can't turn the clock back. And it wouldn't be the way that I remember it anyway."

Tom's friend and fellow former Ranger, Ralph Cacciapaglia, suggested that Tom try riding a dirt bike. Riding has become a lasting habit. "When I am riding on those trails, I can't concentrate on anything but the narrow trail ahead of me," Tom said. "If I don't pay attention I will most likely end up in the trees. Getting out of my own head like that is very therapeutic."

The transition to civilian life is difficult for many veterans. Tom believes that the adjustment would have been significant even if he had not been grievously wounded.

Certain aspects of his new job made the transition even more difficult. "I liked the people that I worked with on my job at HERO Corps and I certainly believed in our mission, but it became extremely frustrating," Tom said. "Sometimes I would find proof of possession—a downloaded image [of child pornography or exploitation]—and a judge would refuse to issue a warrant for further investigation because there was only proof of a single image. In my experience, there was never only a single image. I was constantly infuriated by the slow pace of justice."

Tom's discomfort with the acts he was investigating intensified when he became a father in the autumn of 2017. "After my son was born, I felt as though I could not take looking at what I was looking at and still be an effective father," he said. "I was getting too angry."

"Small Steps"

After trying to set boundaries between work and home, Tom realized he was going to have to find a different way to make a living. "I probably have some PTSD [post-traumatic stress disorder] from my experiences in Afghanistan, but it is nothing compared with the way I was being haunted by the images and information I was seeing online in the course of doing that job," he said. "I saw some truly sick stuff, and it was making me lose some of my faith in humanity, which I am still working to regain."

Tom did make a change. As of this writing, in 2019, he lives in New Hampshire and works on safety and compliance issues for British Aerospace Engineering in New England. He is surprised at how much he likes his nonmilitary job, although he still struggles with certain aspects of the transition back to civilian work and life: "I gave two presentations today, and one of my goals was to not say the word *fuck*," he said. "Small steps."

Tom will need more reconstructive surgery. His right foot still contains six pins and a plate on the first metatarsal. And his nose will continue to need to be rebuilt in order for him to keep breathing clearly.

His vision, of course, is severely limited; he needs to wear glasses and periodically update his Captain America prosthetic eye.

But the life-altering blast has also changed him in a positive way. "I would like to think that I was a pretty good person before the accident, but I think I'm a little more generous now than I was then," Tom said. "I'm friendlier, I'm more patient, and even though I have always tried to motivate the people around me, I feel like I have something different to offer today."

Sometimes Tom is asked to speak with others about dealing with adversity. "I tell them that you need courage to confront adversity, even if the obstacle is personal or domestic," he said. When Tom connects with people who are struggling, he tells them "all the things you don't want to hear when you are at a low point," he said. "But they are true. You are not going to feel like this forever. This feeling will pass. You have to allow yourself to heal. You have to be able to let a little bit go in order to move forward."

Tom has had to let go of a lot, and he believes that "you honor your fallen brothers and sisters by being a good person.

I know I fall short sometimes, but I still try to be a supportive Ranger and to work at being as good a person as I can be."

"When people thank me for my service, part of me wants to laugh," he said. "Being a Ranger is the greatest. I legit signed up so that I could run around and blow stuff up for the rest of my life. I might have romanticized a lot of it before I got there, but I knew what I was getting myself into. The possibility of getting blown up is a risk of going to war."

Like all Rangers, Tom has memorized and reflected on the Ranger Creed. His favorite part is the sixth stanza: "Readily will I display the intestinal fortitude required to fight on to the Ranger objective and complete the mission though I be the lone survivor." "That still resounds after everything," Tom told me. "And recognizing that I volunteered is a big one that follows me to this day. I remind myself that I volunteered for this job, that I loved this job, and that these are the cards that I was dealt. Anything worth having is never free; you have to go out and earn it every day."

EMBRACING THE VALUES
PERSONAL COURAGE

There are different ways to be brave. Personal courage encompasses both physical and moral courage. Moral courage does not necessarily translate into physical courage, and people who are physically brave are not always ethically courageous. But both forms of courage are necessary.

Physical courage is displayed by putting one foot in front of the other. When a soldier is faced with the possibility of death, whether it's because he is going to jump out of an airplane or face down someone with a gun, that soldier exemplifies courage when he jumps anyway, or hoists his weapon and faces the battlefield.

It takes physical courage to be a firefighter rushing into a burning building, to be a police officer going down a dark alleyway toward a screaming civilian, to be an EMT hoisting your gear to the scene of an accident. Our society depends on men and women who are willing to display physical courage in their work. We celebrate the stories of ordinary civilians who display physical courage on behalf of strangers: the guy who stops a robbery in progress by subduing a mugger, or the woman who runs into traffic to pull a wayward toddler back to safety.

We are not as good at celebrating moral courage when we see it, even though we depend on each other to display that kind of bravery in our personal lives. The person who meets unfairness with patience, disappointment with optimism, or adversity with will is displaying moral courage. The person who is willing to confront their own demons and interrupt unhealthy habits and behaviors is displaying moral courage. The people who work to support their families, both financially and emotionally, by putting their loved ones first are displaying moral courage.

Sometimes it requires serious fortitude to resist temptations and put your values first. I'm not saying we should lower the bar to the point where we are congratulating ourselves for fulfilling basic duties and obligations. But it's worth recognizing that it isn't always easy to do the right thing, and certain things are harder for some people than others.

Most people don't need to put their lives on the line when they go to work. But you might need to put yourself in the line of fire to stand up for what is right. You may need to speak up on behalf of the people and values that matter to you. You may need to make sacrifices in order to protect the people and principles that you care about. That takes moral courage, and the more clarity you have about your own values, the easier it will be to be brave.

CHAPTER TEN

FORCES BEYOND US

I N APRIL OF 2009, PIRATES OFF the coast of Somalia captured the American cargo ship *Maersk Alabama*. Many people followed the ordeal of Captain Richard Phillips and his crew, along with the successful rescue effort led by the US Navy, but it is less well known that there were a half a dozen other attempts by pirates to capture ships in the very same week.

Cargo ships, which are quite slow, were becoming increasingly vulnerable to attack. That summer, I was hired as a contractor to provide security for the ships belonging to a company called Pacific-Gulf Marine, Inc.

I flew to Cairo and then drove into Port Suez, a departure point for many cargo ships. These ships moved through the Red Sea like they were on a slow interstate highway through the Arabian Peninsula.

Most routes could be completed in five to ten days, so each journey was relatively brief. I had already had a few trips under my belt that summer when I boarded a boat headed for Cape Town. By this time, I knew that it was normal for pirates to run at us like wolves from their little fiberglass speedboats equipped with huge-ass Yamaha motors.

When we saw a boat like that heading toward us, we—the contractors providing security—would make a point of taking highly visible positions on deck with an M4 or a shotgun. That was usually enough to make a pirate boat change course, and we would watch it turn and roar off.

Imagine a Prius with a V8 engine on it. That is the closest analogy I can make for someone who has never seen one of these boats. Tricked-out boats like the ones the pirates favored can't handle big waves, and they typically stay close to shore, so the cargo ships tended to sail as far from shore as possible without adding to the time it took them to make a delivery.

I tried to schedule my shifts on deck to coincide with sunrises and sunsets. We had some beautiful nights and mornings sailing the Red Sea. I couldn't believe how gorgeous it was, watching the colors of the sky melt into one another before dissolving into the sea.

I also couldn't believe how hot it was, even in the middle of the ocean. I began wearing shorts all the time that summer. Some people got a kick out of the fact that I spent the whole night fighting in Benghazi wearing cargo shorts. I only started wearing shorts on ops after my experience providing security on the cargo ships.

"I Can't Fight Mother Nature"

Once a boat entered the Indian Ocean, the seas would start to churn. The weather had been pretty calm during the first couple of trips I had taken, but we hit some bad weather on this journey, about four days before we were scheduled to reach Cape Town.

As we were sailing past the coast of Somalia, the captain wanted to push farther away from the coast for security reasons, but the seas were unusually heavy. I told him that I'd rather fight pirates than fight those seas. That was the truth. I wasn't scared of getting shot at, and I wasn't scared of a fight, but I can't fight Mother Nature. I was scared of the power of that ocean.

The captain disagreed with me, and it was his call because he was the captain, so we put more distance between our ship and the coast. We got hammered by twenty- and thirty-foot swells for days on our way to South Africa.

I remember going to the highest point on the captain's deck during my shifts and feeling helpless as I looked out at those swells. The waves looked like monsters. We would rise up on them high, and sometimes we would come down light and just rock back and forth, but other times we would come down hard, almost like the ship was hitting concrete.

At one point, we passed a Thai ship that had lost its engines, which really put them at the mercy of the ocean. The ship was being tossed around like a toy boat in a bathtub. We radioed them to see if they needed help and they said they were in the middle of a repair and had it under control, but it made me uneasy to watch them. Even our crew was getting spooked. I knew that the cook and the first mate had made this trip a million times, so it was unsettling to see them act as though we had something to worry about.

For three days, the ocean rolled like this. It was intense, especially at night, like being on a slow roller coaster. I cringed every time we rose up, half expecting the ship to break in half when it came down hard.

Praying for Rain

There wasn't a lot of rain, just heavy waves and wind. The boatman told me that actual rain would help to knock some of the waves down, which was hard to believe, but I started praying for some rain, just in case.

The captain arranged for us to dock in Durban in order to save the additional day it would have taken us to get to Cape Town. Miraculously, the sky opened up and it started raining a few hours before we docked. I quickly discovered that the boatman had been correct; the rain really did seem to knock the waves back, and the sea became calmer for the first time in three days.

As we pulled into Durban, the foul weather broke and turned into sunshine and blue skies.

When ships enter the ports, they are guided in because the ports are so crowded. Another captain is flown out in a helicopter, and he will rope down and guide a ship into an unfamiliar port for the last mile or two.

At that time, Durban was a dangerous place, but from my vantage point on deck during that last mile, it looked like a resort. The sunshine felt surreal and I experienced a peaceful rush as we glided toward the dock on calm waters.

For me, the previous three days of sailing to Durban were more gut-wrenching than getting shot at had ever been. I do not fear men. I can fight men. I can't fight the ocean. I had no control over this display of nature's power, and I had to trust the captain to make the correct decision. In this case, that single decision, whether to stay close to the coast or head farther out into the sea, could have been the difference between life and death. Once that decision was made, there was not much that I could do. After that, I kept my feet on the ground with GRS stuff.

FINDING THE WAY

I remember doing a thirty-mile ruck movement early in my training with the 75th Ranger Regiment, moving quickly through a tropical environment with thick undergrowth. We were learning how to move tactically at a fifteen-minute-per-mile pace with fifty- to seventy-five-pound rucks on our backs and approximately twenty-five additional pounds of gear on our bodies including our weapons systems and ammo. If you try that for yourself, you'll find that the pace is very brisk and the ruck is very heavy.

Most of us were sliding over fallen leaves, tripping over tree roots, and trying to avoid the yellow jackets that were swarming around us.

At some point, I realized that the experienced point leaders seemed to be keeping us on track and moving right through every obstacle without even using a compass. I was just trying to keep up, slipping left and right, and they were gliding confidently forward like it was nothing. How did they know where we were?

Soldiers learn the basics of land navigation during basic training. If you have read my book *The Ranger Way,* you know that I completed infantry basic training twice, once in 1995 the first time I joined the Army and then again in 1999 when I worked hard to get back in. Each time, one of the first things we were taught was how to use a lensatic compass, which is a precision instrument used with a topographic map when someone needs to navigate an area without trails. We also learned how to shoot an azimuth, which requires sighting an object on the horizon in the direction you're traveling and then adjusting the compass heading to make sure you're still moving in the right direction.

In all branches of the military, learning how to read a map and even how to find a map are core skills that need to be mastered from the start. That can be more complicated than it sounds. When most civilians hear the word "map," I'm betting they imagine one big image of a state or a town, and that image encompasses everything in a particular geographic area.

In the Army, the map you are working with might be nothing more than a bunch of coordinates, numbers that coincide with each other. A particular map might cover thousands of square kilometers or only a few hundred.

A map might have contour lines, which can help us figure out out how steep a mountain is before we climb it. If all the contour lines meet and come together? That is a cliff. One map might need to link to another map as though they are puzzle pieces. Soldiers are trained this way because we might need to find our way in the field without much to go on.

When I was on a deployment, it was a priority to really study a map of my location and commit it to memory. An American does not want to get lost in most of the places where I have deployed. When I am deploying, I continually practice my orienteering skills and consider it part of doing my job. I pin maps to the walls and I study them, building a mental picture that I can refer to when I walk or drive. I want to know my north, south, east, and west instinctively, wherever I am, and I want to know some key backstops and landmarks, so that I know if I am going to compound X but I get to bazaar Y, I'll be clear that I've gone too far and I missed it.

When I was walking around on my own in Kabul, I couldn't just pull out a map or my GPS. If you are involved in covert activity, you have to look like you belong. If you are a local, or if you belong in a neighborhood, you don't need a map, right? My job also required a high degree of situational awareness, which is compromised if I have to be bent over a map trying to figure out where I am. I needed to be focused on the environment, not on myself.

Finally, we had to be on alert at all times, and if we got an emergency call, we had to respond as quickly as possible. To that end, we would memorize map tables and all their elements—the contents, the symbols, the colors. If we had time, our team would study a map before a mission and plan together.

In training, once we have been taught how to read different kinds of maps, we learn about grid coordinates. Our instructors would take our unit out to a land navigation range, which is a wooded area that has been studded with metal posts that have orange-and-white boxes on top of them.

The boxes are about ten inches square, and all four sides of the boxes have triangles with numbers on them. You might think that we would be able to see these boxes from a mile away, but we couldn't—they are exposed to the elements of Georgia and they are rarely repainted, so they are not always easy to find. We'd be sent out into the woods with a map, a protractor, and a lensatic compass. We would have five points marked on the map and would be given a time limit to find them.

This activity takes place toward the end of basic training, when the groups should be working well together. No one has to get along; everyone just has to work together. Each group needs to use their map to strategize the best route to get from point A to point B. The shortest distance may not be the best route, depending on the topography of the area.

For example, it might not make sense to cross a marsh and then climb a big-ass hill to get to a box if another route takes longer but gets everyone there on relatively flat, dry land. Point A to D to C to B may be the best route. We had to use our protractors to figure all this out.

Learning How to Walk in a Straight Line

Try to imagine yourself in this situation: you shoot your azimuth, which means you put that compass in your hand, point it north and turn it to figure out which way you want to go. Let's say you have figured out that you need to start walking 152 degrees in a straight line, but guess what? You're in the forest. There are trees in the way. There are rocks. There are ridges and draws. In the woods, it is harder to read the terrain and orient your map than it would be in a city.

Since you can't walk in a straight line, you need a pace count to track your distance. In the military, a pace count is in meters. I knew that every time my right foot hit, that was one meter. At a normal walking pace on flat ground, I cover one hundred meters in sixty-seven steps, counting each step I take on my right foot. So if I need to walk five hundred meters on unobstructed ground, I need to count to sixty-seven five times. While I'm counting, I have to pay attention to my direction, because if have to deviate from my angle in order to go around some obstacle, eventually I will be completely off the 152-degree angle that I determined from my azimuth.

In training, my groups always found this out the hard way.

We always found our points eventually, but it usually took longer than the time we were given, and we would have to reshoot our azimuths and replot our course again and again because we kept drifting to the right. Over time, we got better and learned to trust that compass.

Navigating at night was the hardest for me to learn and become efficient at. I had the worst problems when it was dark out because I would feel like I was going the wrong way, even though I was following the compass. The face of the compass glowed in the dark, and I can remember looking at it and wanting to deviate a little bit because my body just didn't trust it.

I would second-guess the compass, imagining that maybe I had dropped it or busted it up in some way. Second-guessing my training, and my compass, always resulted in my being late to the point. We used to navigate over and over, in all different kinds of terrain, and my skills improved, just as they would have with any other skill repetition. Over time, I developed more confidence in my equipment and stopped trying to outsmart myself.

Navigation skills don't only help you get to where you are going; they can help you get out of a bad situation. I remember an episode in Kabul where some US military intelligence guys got into a car wreck and men who looked like the Afghan police on the scene were trying to yank the US military intelligence guys out of their vehicles.

The US military intelligence guys in that car put out a call on the SAT-COM radio channel that every American unit in the city knew to use to call for a quick reaction force: "We need help, whoever is in the area." I then received a call on my GRS team radio calling all available GRS members to muster in the team room. Our standard operating procedure was to get our weapons, armor, and vehicles and then receive instructions as we were moving toward the location of the unit that needed help. When I got to the team room, four teams had already grabbed their gear and car keys and were shooting out of the gate. I kitted up and headed out with two other team members in a car. It's important to get out of the gate. The worst thing you can do while someone is waiting for assistance is sit and wait for instructions. That is what happened in Benghazi: we were told to wait for instructions on site. In this situation, four teams were already out of the gate, my team was about two minutes behind them, and we all took different routes to converge on the location. As the Afghani police saw the show of force coming in, the cars and men kitted up with gear and rifles, they backed off and let the US Military guys leave their car wreck. The US Military personnel were allowed to leave and no one was injured.

The seed of an effective response to that call lies in everyone's navigation preparation. When someone in trouble gives us their location, there is no time to start from zero figuring out where it is. A lot of the roads in Kabul didn't have names, or they had multiple names for the same roads or intersections, but it didn't matter because I knew the city like the back of my hand. All the good contractors did. We knew the grids and the roads and could respond without needing to look at a map or stop and ask for help.

Some cities or terrains are easier to learn than others. Baghdad is hard to navigate: it is completely flat, so there is usually no terrain to note, and, as in many of the Iraqi cities, it is possible to walk or drive down a road that becomes an alley without warning.

Something may look like a road on a map, but the walls of the buildings come in so close together that nothing wider than a donkey cart could pass through it. I have driven through rows of compounds with eight-foot-high walls in front of them, and I have been in situations where the road I am on just keeps getting narrower as I drive.

I could blink and, all of a sudden, I wouldn't be able to get out of my car if I wanted to, because the walls are too close together for me to open the doors of my car.

The roads are not all paved either, so if the road you are on doesn't have at least a little gravel, it will turn to quicksand every time it gets wet. If it starts to rain while you are driving, it will take no time for your car to get stuck on one of those roads. It doesn't matter if the car is a four-wheeler.

We had a team in town once who didn't know the back roads very well. They were great guys, but I guess they were too full of pride to ask for some basic information from guys who had been there longer. These guys were security on an op, and had a case officer with them. They were driving back to the base on a rainy day, trying to make sure they weren't being followed, and they took a turn down what appeared on the map to be a road, but it turned out to be an alley that narrowed into what might more accurately be described as a walkway.

Stuck in the Mud

Once they figured out how narrow the road was, they went to put the car in reverse, and since it was raining, their car just sank and dug right into the mud. My team, along with two other teams, responded to their call for help. We got the case officer out of there, then switched vehicles and basically stayed out all night, digging them out. Of course, the cars

223

were burned, which means that their identity was compromised because the locals knew they had been associated with Americans, so the cars could no longer be used.

There are a lot of things to worry about when we are working overseas. I understand why people might be tempted to prioritize other vital skills and objectives over basic work like orienteering, but doing so would be a mistake. That team that we dug out of the mud in Baghdad wasn't a bad group, but mistakes can be made, even at a high level.

Preparing for Battle

In 2001, the 75th Ranger Regiment trained in a mountain-city environment in Fort Knox, Kentucky. This was a state-of-the-art facility in which the trainers could simulate battle conditions in a mock city. They could start fires right there, and sometimes they would employ people to act as bystanders during our missions so that we could learn to navigate civilians and protesters, as well as enemies, on the battlefield.

We practiced close-quarter battle techniques, clearing rooms within buildings as a squad and a platoon, techniques to minimize our visibility, or the choreography involved in clearing a building from the bottom up and top down simultaneously without teams shooting each other.

All of our training at this facility culminated in a night op that was considered to be the most challenging one at Fort Knox. Our mission was to locate an enemy and recover a teacher who had been kidnapped. I remember flying in to the scene on a Chinook, as part of a formation, and watching through the open doors of the helicopter as we approached our target.

We were banking it in order to see what was going on, and it was pure chaos on the ground. The mock city was on fire, protesters were rioting, and the sound of the helos was drowning everything else out in my ears.

I had been in on the op order because I was the acting leader for the weapons squad. The op orders are the directions provided by the leadership to coordinate the mission. This was odd for a junior Ranger, since weapons squads usually have the senior squad leader as the leader. My weapons squad leader had recently been promoted to acting platoon sergeant since our platoon sergeant was away at First Sergeant Academy. I was overwhelmed by the responsibility, and even though I was prepared, I did not feel fully prepared for the responsibility that I would hold during this training op.

My job was to provide support, putting up blocking positions as we cleared the buildings so that the line guys could get out with the kidnap victim when they found her. I knew where my teams were supposed to go and how they were supposed to fall out and coordinate so that we could start suppressive fire. I remember feeling somewhat overwhelmed but also knowing that my leaders had faith in me.

I tried to terrain associate from up in the helo to find my building and anticipate where we were going to land. No matter what your team has planned or hoped for, a helicopter may need to come in at a different angle, depending on the conditions in the field. We were aware that we might need to reorient on the ground at a moment's notice.

I found our target building and recognized the area where we landed, so I knew which way to move. Our gun team used a specific method of movement as we approached the building. Another Ranger and I were supposed to get to a particular floor within the building to start the suppressive fire. We were running with our rounds, tripods, and machine guns.

My ammo bearer had an M4, so I put him up front since he would be able to set up faster if we got in trouble.

The platoon sergeant had fast roped with his element onto the top of the building, so they were clearing from the top down. I could hear the platoon sergeant yelling at me over the radio, "Ranger Paronto, where the fuck are you guys at?"

I called back, "Roger, Sergeant. We are linked up. We are moving as fast as we can."

There was fire and smoke everywhere, and the illumination from the fire was whiting out my night-vision goggles, so I raised them off my eyes since they were doing me no good. The civilian protesters were screaming, "Americans, go home!" at us, and even though they spread out when they saw us coming with our guns, they didn't leave the scene.

We had a choice to make about whether to interact with the protesters or just keep an eye on them, which is the kind of call you have to make in real time. We decided to treat them as more of a nuisance and not engage them at the start.

We got in the building and, following our plan, raced up the different stairwells, trying to get our guns in the fight. On the third-floor landing, I met up with one of the leaders of another gun team. He told me that the staircase was not secure, so my team set up our guns in a room right there on the third floor.

We started laying the suppressive fire, shooting only when necessary and making sure not to hit the protesters. The sergeant was screaming at me on the radio, asking why we weren't on the roof. I tried to tell him that we understood that the stairwell was not secure. He didn't respond on the radio, so we finished that stage of the op there.

Over the radio, we got word that our people had taken

out the bad guy and recovered the kidnapped teacher. There was an unexpected twist, which was that the teacher was in a wheelchair and unable to walk. She had been recovered in the same building that we were in, and, at that point, our job was to make sure that no one else got into the building while the rescue team was getting her out.

The building was large, six floors with fifty-meter hallways all around. I could see the blacked-out lights of the returning helos with my infrared vision through the windows. Our teams were moving back toward the birds at their predetermined positions.

We were blocking, holding a clear path and providing security for the team to come out with the schoolteacher. As they exited the building, the protesters started to group together, so we tried to provide some security for the squad leader who was pushing the wheelchair.

"Start Pushing, Ranger!"

Somehow, this squad leader had managed to lead the charge to the helo and was pushing the schoolteacher in a wheelchair right in front—with no cover.

We started running hard to get a gun up front and cover this guy. Remember, this is a training op, so people are going to make mistakes. By the time we got through this complete chaos and saw the ramp of the Chinook coming down, I was smoked as hell.

The schoolteacher got wheeled on, we did a quick headcount, the ramp went up, and we took off, leaving the city still burning below in the distance. The sensation of sweeping up away into the sky after an op never gets old, even an op that was for training.

My peace of mind was short-lived. The acting platoon sergeant was waiting for me when we got off the Chinook. The first words I heard were, "Start pushing, Ranger!" I immediately dropped to the ground with my face to the floor and started doing push-ups while he yelled at me.

"Why didn't you get to the top of that building?"

"We were told...," I started, but he cut me off.

"You should have found another way to get to me," he said. "Keep pushing."

I kept pushing and I didn't complain. Another sergeant, Hopkins, came over and asked what was going on. I continued doing push-ups as the two leaders conferred with one another.

The truth is that I had had a job to do and I didn't do what I needed to do from where I was supposed to do it. I didn't get up to the top. I was thinking about how else I might have gotten there and whether we should have disobeyed Leonard and cleared the stairwell ourselves.

Before I had sorted it out, Hopkins—a big, soft-spoken guy and an outstanding leader—told me to get up. "Dude, you did good," he told me. "Get out of here."

EMBRACING THE VALUES
KEEP THE FAITH

My life changed when I returned to the United States after Benghazi. I felt betrayed by my government when the events of September 11, 2012, became politicized.

Many people were surprised that I wanted to continue working to defend Americans, and that I could still feel patriotic after what our team survived. But I have never lost faith in my brothers and I have never lost faith in the people of our country.

The truth is that if I could be my old self again, deploying and not doing any public speaking, I think I would go back in time. But I accept that I have been put on a new path. I believe that my story, and the stories of other patriots, have something to teach people, something that many Americans seem to need to hear right now. I know that listening to their stories helps me to be a better man.

I am still uncomfortable speaking in public. Sharing the story of our night fighting in Benghazi is emotionally draining. There have been moments during the last few years when I have been sorely tempted to quit. But if sharing the story of my experience in Benghazi corrects the historical record and keeps the memory of Tyrone Woods and Glen Doherty alive, it's worth it. If I can bring attention to the stories of other men and women who serve and the issues that we care about, it's worth it. If something in one of our stories resonates with a stranger and helps another person make a positive change in their own life, it's worth it.

When I muster the courage to tell people about the ways that I have struggled and failed, I can see that it makes an impression, particularly in a time when many people go to great lengths to curate identities on social media that are perfect, enviable—and false.

I still struggle, but I try to stay positive, grateful for my second chances, and mindful of how I am using them. When I listen to the stories of other people who have sacrificed to protect our country, I am humbled. They help me put my own obstacles into perspective. They also make me proud to be an American.

There are many different ways to serve, and you need to have faith that you will come to know yours. If there is anything in these pages that causes you to reflect on your own values, that helps you to find your own mission, that brings you comfort or hope, or that helps you to appreciate the blessings of your citizenship, then I will feel grateful that I am continuing to serve. Our nation is stronger when we are all willing to sacrifice and to work hard to be the best possible version of ourselves. Never quit.

GIVE AND GET HELP

FREEDOM IS NOT FREE. The stories of sacrifice that are gathered in these pages are just a few examples of the price that some Americans pay for our freedom and security. One of my priorities is to honor individuals—and their families—who have sacrificed to protect the United States.

Military personnel and first responders can routinely find themselves in tragic and violent situations as part of their work. The unique circumstances of that work can make it challenging to transition back to civilian life and, for some people, can lead to physical and emotional struggles that put people at risk of isolation, despair, and even suicide.

The men and women who put their lives on the line for this country deserve our very best efforts. The organizations listed below honor some of our fallen heroes and provide support for active service members, their families, veterans, and law enforcement personnel.

Please consider supporting their work in any way that you

can. If you are a veteran in need, I encourage you to reach out to any of these organizations for support or as a starting point to finding other help. You are not alone.

14TH HOUR FOUNDATION

https://14thhourfoundation.nationbuilder.com/

I helped found the 14th Hour Foundation to honor and support veterans, first responders, military contractor personnel, and the families of those who have served and sacrificed to protect the American homeland. These individuals and their families often have unexpected needs in the months and years following a related injury or death that government programs do not cover. The fund provides honor grants to these individuals and their immediate families when they need them and to other charitable organizations that provide veteran support services and promote awareness of these needs.

ARMY RANGER LEAD THE WAY FUND

leadthewayfund.org

The Army Ranger Lead the Way Fund works directly with the US Special Operations Care Coalition to address and support the ongoing needs of Army Rangers and their families beyond what the government can offer.

THE GLEN DOHERTY MEMORIAL FOUNDATION

www.glendohertyfoundation.org

The Glen Doherty Memorial Foundation was established to honor Bub by assisting current and former special operations professionals and their families with the transition to civilian life by supporting educational and recreational opportunities for service members and their families.

THE TYRONE SNOWDEN WOODS WRESTLING FOUNDATION

www.tyronewoodswrestlingfoundation.org

Tyrone Woods was a champion high school wrestler for Oregon City High School and a state champion of the Oregon State Wrestling Association in 1989. This foundation honors Rone by providing financial, educational, and charitable support to high school wrestlers and wrestling programs in Oregon.

OPERATION VETERAN OUTDOORS

Operationveteranoutdoors.com

Israel Matos, whom you read about in this book, is the president of Operation Veteran Outdoors (OVO). Based in Florida, OVO helps veterans cope with their combat-related injuries and PTSD by organizing events where those veterans can interact with other warriors who have been through similar life experiences and injuries. OVO gives these warriors the opportunity to express themselves among their peers and share the camaraderie that they experienced while in the service. OVO also connects these veterans to other resources and programs as appropriate.

PJ PARARESCUE FOUNDATION

www.pararescuefoundation.org

I'm always surprised that more people don't know about the pararescue community. These warriors are uniquely trained to recover isolated and injured people in hazardous conditions, provide emergency medical care, and bring them home. This is the only organization that is exclusively devoted to supporting and addressing the needs of US Air Force pararescue and combat rescue officer service members, veterans, and their families.

SGT RYAN E. DOLTZ MEMORIAL FOUNDATION INC

rememberingryan.org

The Doltz family established this foundation to honor the memory of the late Sergeant Ryan Doltz, whom you read about in this book. The foundation makes donations to military families in need of assistance and to other organizations that provide services to military families. It has established scholarships in Ryan's name at the Virginia Military Institute and at Dover High School, Ryan's alma mater; a scholarship for a college-bound student from Morris County, New Jersey; and a scholarship for the education of a member or dependent of the New Jersey National Guard.

THE UNITED SERVICE ORGANIZATIONS (USO)

www.uso.org

The USO has been providing resources, programs, and entertainment to service members, veterans, and their families since World War II. Today, it provides services at 160 locations around the world. Many people think that the USO is a government agency because it works closely with the Department of Defense, but it is a nonprofit, charitable corporation established by Congress that relies on volunteers and private donations. The USO plays an important role in keeping service members connected to their families. After September 11, 2012, I was flown from Benghazi to Tripoli and then to Germany with not much more than the clothes on my back. The USO took very good care of me.

SFC ALWYN C. CASHE DESERVES THE MEDAL OF HONOR
facebook.com/groups/264150296957437

I encourage you to visit Harry Conner's public Facebook page devoted to Alwyn Cashe. The site is not a fund-raiser, but it is dedicated to SFC Cashe's memory. You can read more here about Sergeant Cashe's life, as well as support and monitor the efforts being made to secure the Medal of Honor for his selfless sacrifice.

ACKNOWLEDGMENTS

I AM GRATEFUL for many colleagues and friends that I can't name, both in the 75th Ranger Regiment and in other parts of the military and contracting world. They don't always get the recognition they deserve. My great friend and fellow contractor John Borg kept me sane on long deployments away from home and then after my return home after the events of September 11, 2012. I wouldn't be on this earth without his support and continued friendship.

Tom Block, Scott Gearen, Rob Jaber, Israel Matos, and Ben Morgan allowed me to share some of the toughest parts of their lives in these pages. Cheryl Doltz and the entire Doltz family opened their home to me and shared Ryan's story. James Ryan generously shared his memories of Alwyn Cashe and helped me to understand his extraordinary story. I hope that readers find their stories inspiring. Ben Morgan also provided thoughtful counsel in helping me think through and organize this project, and Melissa Moore helped me execute it.

ACKNOWLEDGMENTS

Thank you to Kate Hartson, Thomas Watkins, the entire team at Hachette, and to Richard Abate and Rachel Kim at 3Arts for their continued interest and support. I'm grateful to Mitchell Zuckoff, our coauthor on *13 Hours*, for getting me started on the writing path.

My family has been a blessing. I'm lucky to have the support of my brother, Mike, and my sister, Jamie, and our parents, Rita and Jim Paronto. The memory and example of my grandparents, Joaquin and Rose Garcia, still guides us all.

My beautiful wife, Tanya, is my best motivation to keep coming back to my values, and our three wonderful children are the best of me. I am grateful to all of them.

Kris "Tanto" Paronto is a former Army Ranger from 2nd Battalion, 75th Ranger Regiment, and a private security contractor who has deployed to South America, Central America, the Middle East, and North Africa. He is the coauthor, with Mitchell Zuckoff and the five surviving security team members, of the *New York Times* bestselling book *13 Hours*, describing his experiences responding to the 2012 terrorist attack on the US Special Mission in Benghazi, Libya, and the author of the *USA Today* bestselling book *The Ranger Way*, in which he shares stories from his training experiences as an Army Ranger and how the lessons he learned can be applied to civilians in search of discipline, motivation, success, and peace in their lives.